MY *Soul's*
BEEN ANCHORED

FOREWORD BY MAYA ANGELOU

MY *Soul's* BEEN ANCHORED

A PREACHER'S *Heritage* IN THE FAITH

H. BEECHER HICKS JR.

Author of *Preaching Through a Storm*

ZondervanPublishingHouse

Grand Rapids, Michigan

A Division of HarperCollinsPublishers

My Soul's Been Anchored
Copyright © 1998 by Kerygma Associates, Inc.

Requests for information should be addressed to:

📖 ZondervanPublishingHouse
Grand Rapids, Michigan 49530

Library of Congress Cataloging-in-Publication Data

Hicks, H. Beecher.
    My soul's been anchored : a preacher's heritage in the faith / H. Beecher Hicks, Jr.
        p.   cm.
    Includes bibliographical references.
    ISBN 0-310-22136-6 (hardcover : alk. paper)
    1. Afro-Americans—Religion.   2. Hicks, H. Beecher.   I. Title.
BR563.N4H54 1998
286'.1'092—DC21   98–10395
                                                    CIP

This edition printed on acid-free paper and meets the American National Standards Institute Z39.48 standard.

Interior design by Jody DeNeef

Printed in the United States of America

---

98 99 00 01 02 03 04 /❖ DC/ 10 9 8 7 6 5 4 3 2 1

To Liz and Kristin
Always home alone . . . waiting!

*My heart was hot within me,
while I was musing the fire burned . . . !*

PSALM 39: 3

CONTENTS

FOREWORD
by Maya Angelou

The African-American preacher is a poet because he has had to be a poet. It was never sufficient that he study the religious canon, or put to memory its precepts and then distribute its laws intact to a willing congregation. From the days of slavery, he (and later, she) had to take the biblical stories and relate them to the present life conditions of the congregants. Thus, in the songs "Go Down Moses," "Didn't My Lord Deliver Daniel," and "Deep River," there is evidence of the use of the Old Testament and New Testament stories as metaphors for slavery and its aftermath of discrimination and inequality.

The preacher has had to use persuasive declamation to convince the nonbeliever and to enhearten the faithful. Few listeners are able to withstand the pull of the good Baptist preacher's voice as it cascades over the congregation and comes to rest in the attentive ear. The mellifluous musical sound can console the broken spirit and soothe the irate heart.

When the sermon is inspired by more than musical talent and grandiloquent language, the result is poetry with a purpose. And so we have it here in H. Beecher Hicks' unusual book, *My Soul's Been Anchored*.

A third-generation African-American preacher, Hicks sets out on the same journey his grandfather took decades ago—that is, "to save the world." Hicks has lived a life ministering to flocks from New York to Texas to Washington, D.C., and his reputation informs that his aim remains the same as that of his ancestor and he has pursued his intent with this volume.

Here he has used prose and poetry to awaken or reawaken faith in his readers. He admonishes and cajoles, warns and promises. He remembers growing up with devout and devoted parents who employed love, well-worn adages, and the occasional "strapping" as necessary implements in the raising of a child.

Humor has long been an important factor in the African-American community. Whether it is used as a disguise, "I laughed to keep from crying," or for its rich release alone, there is no level, class, no state of African-American life without humor.

Hicks uses a subtle turn of phrase or an outright comical situation to lighten the load of this book, heavy with its intent to "save the world."

African-Americans have survived an unspeakable history of horror with the passion and purpose of good preachers and committed ministers.

When I read Hicks' *My Soul's Been Anchored*, I picture a man slave in the early 1800s cutting cane in the devouring fire of a summer sun, his back glowing with a heat which cannot be shifted even when the dark comes.

When I read Hicks' *My Soul's Been Anchored*, I imagine a Black woman during America's depression who had by hand laundered another family's dirty linen and scrubbed another woman's floor, nursing another's babe. I imagine her leaning against a wall or resting against a tree until dark comes.

When I read Hicks' *My Soul's Been Anchored*, I envision a politician in the 1990s duly elected, yet whose small temporal power so threatens the power structure that vast machineries are erected to topple the leader from the earned perch in full view of a scornful world, especially as dark comes.

Hicks wrote:

> And in those moments when the night comes . . .
>   and there are no friends to be found
> when the night comes . . .
>   and your head is "bowed beneath your knees"
> when the night comes . . .
>   and the tranquillity of your home is disturbed. . .
>   the state of your health is suddenly imbalanced
>   your future is grim and your fortune has slipped
>   through your fingers . . .
>   your ship has come in with no cargo on board,
> when the night is upon you

and it is "blacker than a hundred midnights
   down in a cypress swamp,"
you and I need...
in that moment...
a night light, a light in dark places.

. . .

Our ancestors, yours and mine, were much smarter
than are we. They knew that their survival and that of generations to come would depend upon the availability of a
night light. That's why they said so often, "Jesus is a Light
in Dark Places."

. . .

I cannot escape the reality—nor do I wish to—that
I cannot endure the anxiety of the darkness of this world
without a light. What is needed is more than a night light:
The Light. I thank God that there is a Light:

"And the city had no need of the sun,
neither of the moon, to shine in it;
for the glory of the Lord did lighten it,
and the Lamb is the light thereof."

The remark is made in an old spiritual, "My soul looks back
and wonders how I got over." We have "got over," are getting
over, and shall get over, with the passion and persistence of
preachers like Hicks who have taken as their charge that they are
here to save the world.

They have offered us Jesus Christ to help us carry the burden
of inequality, poverty, and racial discrimination. They have given
us Jesus Christ as a light unto our path, on the rocky road of lynch-
ing, of being the last hired and the first fired.

They have given us the healing thought that we live in the
imagination of God.

And there we are, free at last. At last, even when the dark
comes.

PREFACE
by Dr. Allen Dwight Callahan

Assistant Professor of New Testament, Harvard Divinity School

Dr. Hicks is a person whose vocation it is to wrestle with the written word. Three remarkable volumes have already issued from his study, and should he (and we) be so blessed, more may follow. The present volume is yet another remarkable work.

Another Preacher once opined that of the making of books there is no end, but literary fecundity has never been something to take for granted in African American religion. Of course, African Americans have produced literate, even erudite ministers of the Gospel. And some of these ministers wrote books: memoirs, commentaries, essays, histories, and other works in other genres. It could be argued that, historically, a disproportionate number of black intellectuals—that is, people who think and influence the thinking of others through their writings—have been clergy people. But the unlettered men and women of the pulpit loom large in the collective memory of black America. The historic struggle of African Americans to read and write, often inspired by the desire to read the Bible for themselves, is heartrending and heroic. One consequence of their late but speedy entry into the world of letters is that black folks often "got religion," and kept it, before enjoying the blessings of reading, 'riting, and 'rithmetic. Sojourner Truth's preaching, though powerfully prophetic, was necessarily by ear; as she said of her biblical knowledge, "I can't read, but I can hear." Long after Emancipation, folktales were still told about people like "Preacher Bird," an illiterate slave who was set free to pursue his vocation after his master heard him preach. Such is the lore that commemorates the unlettered people of African American religion, illiterates sometimes called from behind the mule to be the next local Moses. Ralph Ellison once claimed that the religion of black folks was so free of the constraints of the written word that they, though Christian, are not "a people of the book." "Our expression," he said, "has been oral as against literary." This from a man who left off a promising career as a jazz musician to pursue a brilliant life of letters.

H. Beecher Hicks Jr. is a virtuoso of one of the world's most demanding oratorical forms, traditional African American preaching. Yet he is an earnestly literate man. A past master of the spoken word, he is at home in the universe of writing and writers. Perhaps this is because he has a special sympathy for the craft. Dr. Hicks composes the texts of his sermons sentence by sentence, syllable by syllable, and delivers them, word for word, with a care and lucidity that may scarcely be heard among the finest lectures in academe. Truly remarkable! But even more so is this: Though he invests his sermons with all the preparation of a brilliant lecture, H. Beecher Hicks Jr. is not a lecturer. No, far, far from it.

The word "lecture" and its cognates have fallen on hard times in contemporary American language. It is a bad thing to be said to "lecture" anybody about anything. This is true everywhere but on the campus and, these days, occasionally true even there. Traditionally among black Baptists, that title is positively a term of opprobrium in the church. To call a preacher a "lecturer"—to describe his sermon by saying, "he lectures" (or, as it is more often and more derisively put, "he just lectures")—is to pronounce his preaching anathema. A "lecturer" is a preacher who can't preach, can't "tell the story"; this condemnation suggests that the preacher so condemned serves up the Gospel proclamation—the "solid food," as St. Paul calls it—like meat without gravy: tough, tasteless, and very, very dry. And in African American preaching, as in African American cuisine, to serve the main meal without gravy is—well, it's just not done. Worst of all, to say that the preacher has "lectured" further suggests that his delivery is not fluid and free. He doesn't recite, he doesn't resound; he reads—the text of the Bible and then the text of his sermon. He has written out beforehand what he preaches and limps along on the crutches of his manuscript. He is free only of eloquence. Thought but no thunder; notes but no music; or, more aptly, grits but no gravy. He is a preacher who cannot "preach." He "just lectures."

H. Beecher Hicks Jr. never, ever "just lectures." No lecturer, he. From his pulpit, the text of his sermon becomes an event. We can esteem his manuscript a crutch only if we can consider the Lindy Hop limping. From a masterpiece of a manuscript he recites his text, thunderously and musically. He moves, the congregation moves, the Spirit moves, and all are swept up in the power of the word which, like the Word that is its source, is both written and heard. And it, too, is powerful and sharper than any two-edged sword. And here we encounter what is truly remarkable. Dr. Hicks gracefully transcends, in Ellison's words, the oral as against the literary. In his preaching and writing we experience the balanced mastery of the written and spoken word in the proclamation of the Word—so skillful and compelling a use of the letter that it does not kill but gives life.

Dr. Hicks has made a distinguished career of illumining the oracles of life. Here he illumines the oracles of his own life and recounts in stirring, touching prose its quiet revelations. Here is the philosophical without sophistry, the sermon without sermonizing. He shares with us his wisdom, his "joy and dread," by inviting us, with a genuine, engaging humility, to sit with him "on the porch of [his] experience." The finely crafted vignettes that await the reader in *My Soul's Been Anchored* are yet more testimony to H. Beecher Hicks Jr.'s gift for weaving together life and letters into the fabric of his text, a text upon which he has labored sentence by sentence, syllable by syllable, and delivers, word for word, with a flourish and fire that have made him one of the great preachers of our time.

INTRODUCTION

$\mathscr{R}$are and precious are those moments when we chance upon an opportunity to reflect on the spiritual experiences of a lifetime. We become so absorbed with "doing" ministry that we fail to journal the oracles of God in our lives; we fail to be responsive to the gentle nudgings, the inner urgings, that "still, small voice."

Albert Einstein once suggested that God's greatest gift to man or woman is not science but imagination ... the simple yet sacred gifts of the visionary: creativity, invention, innovation—imagination. The stored memories of my childhood, when opened, bring again to mind those wonderful, intimate moments when imagination was my one and only companion. In many ways it appears that memory is the storehouse, the keeper of imagination. It all seems so insignificant and innocent now but I remember those nights, stretched out on my bed, the house quiet and still, entertaining myself with

dancing silhouettes created by the street light,
   the sweet whistle of air
created by the wind through the transom,
the moonlight melody of street noises,
bowing branches just outside the window
or the gentle movements of Mama's curtains,
   freshly hung from the wood-frame stretcher
she put up in the kitchen.

I even had musical accompaniment emanating from
an orchestra of honking horns,
ambulance sirens,
bugs aflutter,
brakes screeching—
a veritable symphony of "things that go bump in the night."
These are days of sacred memory for me.

In our younger years, imagination was quite likely defined as "freedom." In our adult years, the memory of that freedom, that imagination, can only be defined as "sacred." These are days when I recall the sacrament of that sacred gift—the imagination of memory's store.

Have you ever imagined something? I have. More important, do you know that it's quite all right to imagine? Imagination is one of God's little extras. It's yours for free, to use when you want and nobody will know. Imagination permits you to look within, to marvel at what you find, to laugh and to be joyous just because God made you *you*. Imagination is just a little secret between you and God.

Imagination is clearly linked to "image"—we are created in the image of God. Who we are, what we are, what we may become is limited only by the plan and design, the "imag[e]-ination" of God. We are rooted, indeed anchored, in God's imagination. Whatever I become is only limited by what God has planned, what God has designed, what God has *imagined* for me. The miracle is that the same God who "imaged" you and me gave us the power to image and imagine on our own.

In many ways I am free if my imagination is free. Despite the artificial boundaries that often constrict life, my imagination becomes the signature of my freedom as it opens to me, as Howard Thurman would suggest, the "sense of options" that mark my peculiar personhood. Imagination is free to be used at will, free to be held fast or revealed, free to be kept secret in the sanctuary of the soul. Because of the imagination that God gives, I have a vision of things that never were and a re-vision of things as they may yet become.

I am able to see beyond the moment if only I can look through the lenses of imagination.

I am able to look within and marvel at my discoveries.

I am able to laugh and rejoice because God has given this gift— uncloned, unduplicated, holding the key to a gift God has given to no other.

I am able to create new worlds,
  conceive new ideas,
  give birth to new inventions,
  spawn renaissance thinking,
  become a better "image" of God,

and come closer to an understanding of who God is,
if only I will use God's gift of imagination.

The meditations and testimonies, quiet thoughts, "experienced experiences" that I relate in this volume are not imaginary. The persons, places, events, and circumstances are real. My intention is to honor the sacred memory of those whose names appear in this book. I know they will be pleased to be a part of this unusual form of Good News expression. I trust that those family members and friends and all who read this work will recognize the love with which I tell these stories. Although the stories contain much that is personal concerning my family and me, I hope the telling will not be interpreted as personal arrogance. It is my hope that you the reader will not only enjoy these writings but will find them of some benefit on your spiritual journey. It is also my hope that you will, through the use of your own imagination, see, hear, and experience the wonderful gifts of imagination that God has similarly made available to you.

Through these pages I have made a necessarily feeble effort to peek into the "imagination" of God–taking a microscopic look to see God's truth, to envision God's deeper meanings, and to understand the purpose of God's imaginings–examining the life of the Spirit and the life of the church.

Imagination–my storehouse of wonderful "collectibles" that are reflected here–must do honor to the sacred memory of those whose names appear in this volume. Where would I be were it not for the nurturing influence of the people of God at the Mount Olivet Baptist Church of Columbus, Ohio; the Second Baptist Church of Mumford, New York; the Mount Ararat Baptist Church of Pittsburgh, Pennsylvania; and the Antioch Missionary Baptist Church of Houston, Texas? Their lives and stories have intersected with and enriched my life in ways that neither they nor I could ever have imagined.

You alone will judge the value of this work and determine its spiritual appropriation. *My Soul's Been Anchored* is, in many ways, a reflection of my own spiritual journey, the telling of my never-ending walk with God. Perhaps as you journey through these pages you will chance upon the familiar–some person, event, or place that recalls to your mind that sacred gift of imagination and memory. Or perhaps you will encounter the living Christ through the eyes of yet another seeker after truth.

The persons (both friends and enemies), the experiences recalled, the insights gained over thirty-six years of preaching the Gospel of Jesus Christ, and my romance with the reading, hearing, teaching, and preaching of the Word have forged the anchor of grace and mercy that has held me fast in days of sunshine and nights of storm. The consequence of it all is a compendium of my spiritual journey, a record of those elements of my life that have stabilized and secured me. You must understand that these writings do not come from human initiative alone; there is another source, a source of power that comes from a yielded life, a life called out and sent forth, a life prompted by the hand of the Divine. God's Word formed and forged the solid anchor that holds me steadfast and unmovable even in the midst of the storm; God lifts my eyes to see the shining Son.

> *I surrender to God the nerve center of my consent. This is the very core of my will, the mainspring of my desiring, the essence of my conscious thought. . . .*
>
> *These are the things I reserve for my innermost communion; these are the fires that burn on the various altars of my life; these are the outreaches of my spirit enveloping all the hurt, the pains, the injustices and the cruelties of life.*
>
> *These are the things by which I live and carry on.*[1]

Please forgive any inaccuracies of date, place, or time in this book. I am deeply indebted to the members of the Metropolitan Baptist Church, the flock of God I am privileged to serve at present; thank you, my friends, for the time you so generously gave me to compile and complete this work. To the members of my staff who kept the fires burning and have assisted in the preparation, editing, and final drafting my gratitude is full and real. In addition, this work could not have been completed except for the loving yet critical reviews given by Dr. Genna Rae McNeil of the University of North Carolina and by my colleague in ministry, the Reverend Jeffrey Haggray of the Mount Gilead Baptist Church of

Washington, D. C. I have been blessed by the constant encouragement and literary assistance of Mrs. Bebe Coker. Finally, to my family, "always waiting at home," my gratitude for understanding my need to move beyond the "doing" of ministry to live in the imagination of God—if only for a moment.

PART *One*

IMAGINE
BEGINNINGS

Precious is the soil in which we have been planted, taken root, and blossomed. We are nothing at all if not a reflection of the place of our beginnings, the circumstances out of which we have come, the fruit of the pruning and cultivation of persons and events that have come into our lives. Our beginnings constitute the anchor of our souls.

From time to time I have been accused—rightfully so—of resisting the present because of my reverence for the past. They tell me that I long for the ancient; they suggest that I have been misplaced in the wrong century. I gladly accept the accusation. The context of my speech, the images of my mind, the fundamentals of my theology have been framed by those persons and events of yesterday who, in my view, ought be the paradigm for life today. I do not suppose that my experience is normative for others; it provides for me, however, that certain and sure anchor of integrity and truth that holds fast in the swirling winds of a chaotic culture.

Someone has said that the plans we have for our lives are really documented imagination. God has a plan for our lives that permits us to participate in God's creative activity. Because we are literally created in the image(ination) of God, we have so much more potential, so much more opportunity to be all that we want to be, to be more than is visible even to ourselves. If it is true that all we see was originally a thought in the mind of God, I wonder what God thought for us? My life is stable and secure only when anchored in the imagination of God.

Whither shall I go from thy spirit? or whither shall I flee from thy presence? If I ascend up into heaven, thou art there: if I make my bed in hell, behold, thou art there. If I take the wings of the morning, and dwell in the uttermost parts of the sea; Even there shall thy hand lead me, and thy right hand shall hold me.

PSALM 139:7-10

IN A LONELY PLACE

There is a loneliness about this place ... this place of my choosing. Surrounded by the things of life, I have suddenly come face to face with the solitariness of life. One person, one life, one place, one God, one moment in time—solitary, alone, yet not alone.

God has chosen his way of filling this place and this space in my life with the "ordinariness" of life. How long has it been since I lost the sense of the wondrous, magnificent works of God? How long has it been since I have been excited about what God is doing before my very eyes? How long has it been since God became ordinary?

How strange that the sun should become ordinary to me, that
    clouds,
    and rain,
    and snow,
    and sunshine
have become common, pedestrian fare.
How strange that God should choose to speak through naked branches having
    neither bud
    nor bloom,
that God should choose to utter sounds
    through rivers and streams
        frozen in place,
        in icicles glittering
promises of still more winter, still more discontent.
Or that God should choose

to brave speaking
through the commonplace roads of my existence
and has made them
icy, slippery, impassable, treacherous ...
sending me off in unknown directions, sliding,
sometimes falling,
meeting new hurt—in peculiar places.
How strange of God
to speak through the ordinariness of life.
How strange.

I do not know just why I am here. I do not know what I am to do here. More to the point, I do not know how I got to this place, which is so far from where I started out, so far from the destination to which I was determined to go. I only know that I must follow that Voice, the Voice that speaks in tones that I am familiar with, tones that I have so often failed to listen to and failed often to understand or obey.

Could it be that I am in this lonely place, this solitary space, to wait again for the Empowering Presence?

... to wait again for the Call that I alone am burdened to hear?

... to wait again for that purifying,

energizing, frightening fire that burns within?

I need to feel it again. I need to know that God's fire is my fire. I desperately need to know that my loneliness is not permanent and that my solitariness is filled with the awesome purposefulness of God.

This moment, this hour, this time is not mine, it belongs to God. I am now wholly alone, wholly vulnerable, wholly available. Come, Holy Spirit, with wind and fire. Let your breath blow anew in my life. Penetrate my soul and my personality with the power of your touch. Broken, humbled, frightened, unsure of today and tomorrow ... only sure that you are there. Come, Holy Spirit, use me now! Let the fire burn!

I pray that out of his glorious riches he may strengthen you with power through his Spirit in your inner being, so that Christ may dwell in your hearts through faith. And I pray that you, being rooted and established in love, may have power, together with all the saints, to grasp how wide and long and high and deep is the love of Christ, and to know this love that surpasses knowledge—that you may be filled to the measure of all the fullness of God.

Now to him who is able to do immeasurably more than all we ask or imagine, according to his power that is at work within us, to him be glory in the church and in Christ Jesus throughout all generations, forever and ever! Amen.

EPHESIANS 3:16-21 NIV

LIVING IN THE IMAGINATION OF GOD

I wonder if God wonders. I wonder if God dreams. I wonder if God imagines. If God wonders, I wonder what the imagination of God must be! Vast. Enormous. Incomprehensible. The awesome imagination of God!

Not long ago, I caught myself doing something I rarely do. I actually took a moment to daydream. I cannot remember when last I actually had the time—or the inclination—to daydream. I honestly cannot remember when last I allowed myself this luxury, this blessedness of idleness.

When is the last time you allowed yourself just to be free, open, idle, yet completely susceptible to the winds of the moment, permitting any thought at all to invade your mental space?

... to daydream of things that used to be, the "good ol' days" that, in reality, were not really as "good" as you imagined them to have been.

... to daydream of school days and playground pranks, of secrets shared ... and kept ... and lost, of things that made you laugh in years past, and then to know that sacred, secret laughter once again.

... to daydream of what my mother called the "almost nearly but not quite" experiences of life. How different, how much more adventuresome, how much more exciting life would have been if it could have been even nearly (but not quite) as you planned it, or schemed it, or dreamed it so many, many years ago.

... to daydream of tomorrows delayed.

Where is that tomorrow with its promise of Rudyard Kipling's "impostors"—success, fortune, and wealth?

Where is that tomorrow where dreams become realities and where hopes are never falsely revived, only to die again?

Where is that tomorrow?

Where is that ultimate tomorrow with pieces of the puzzle that always fit?

Where the crisis is over, before it even starts ... the pain—gone; tears—dried?

Tomorrow is caressed;

even now—in the imagination of God....

Where is that tomorrow?

I still wonder if God wonders. I still wonder what God imagines for me. I wonder if my name is ever mentioned in the daydreams of God. For all of my wondering, for all of my daydreams, for all of my imaginings, I can never fully *imagine* what God *imagines.* I just wonder....

> *Such knowledge is too wonderful for me;*
> *it is high, I cannot attain unto it.*

PSALM 139:6

Thanks be to God that he has the capacity to imagine far beyond the limitations and boundaries of my daydreams.

Thanks be to God for redefining the concept; when I have come to the end of my understanding of the possible, God redefines the thought and offers to me the potential of moving to a realm of the Divine that only God and I can ever know.

Thanks be to God for never imagining me collectively. Thanks be to God for imagining the singular me.
God has something in mind for me.
God wants something *for me.*
God has something in store just *for me.*
God provides the unexpected
with the most peculiar precision—
    just for me.
"God so loved the world
that He gave His only begotten Son . . . !"
    just for me.

And in this world God seeks to respond to the needs, the desires, the daydreams—yours and mine. God loves me so much that God imagines for me!

> *"For I know the plans I have for you," declares the LORD, "plans to prosper you and not to harm you, plans to give you hope and a future."*
>
> JEREMIAH 29:11 NIV

Can you possibly imagine that much love? God loves me so much that He "imagines" just for me! And because God loves me I want to live holy, wholly, solely, completely in the wondrous love, in the imagination of God. I want to let God's power work in me and give me the power to do more than I can imagine for me and more than I can imagine for my children and my children's children. I imagine a life so deeply wrapped up and tangled up in the Spirit that God will be able to use my dreams, use my visions, use my imagination as instruments of His presence in the world. Never let me stray from the imagination of God.

I wonder if God wonders, I wonder if God imagines. I am content to live my life and leave my life in the hands of an imagining God.

> *Now to him who by his power within us is able to do infinitely more than we ever dare to ask or imagine—to him be glory in the Church and in Jesus Christ for ever and ever, amen!*
>
> EPHESIANS 3:20 PHILLIPS

In the beginning God created the heaven and the earth. . . . And God said, Let us make man in our image, after our likeness: and let them have dominion over the fish of the sea, and over the fowl of the air, and over the cattle, and over all the earth. . . .

GENESIS 1:1, 26

In the beginning was the Word, and the Word was with God, and the Word was God. . . . In him was life; and the life was the light of men.

JOHN 1:1, 4

THE PLACE OF BEGINNING

Do you remember the place of your beginning? I mean, really remember where it all began for you?

Close your eyes.

Squeeze tight, now!

How much do you really remember?

Do you remember your first encounter with

the wind or the rain in your face?

Do you remember

your backyard swing where every day you stretched to touch the clouds with your toes?

your first ice cream cone on a hot Sunday afternoon?

It's sort of aggravating when your tongue's not long enough to catch the drip on your chin!

Do you remember the first house you lived in? Where the floorboards creaked? Your secret hiding place? Can you close your eyes and still make your way from room to room?

Careful now, watch out for your mother's "what not" shelf!

What about the faces? Do you remember the faces of those you loved? Do you remember the faces of those who loved you first?

I pulled my car down the freshly paved road. I was driving a rental car, but even so it was a kind of triumphal return—a kind of

31

"native son come home." It had been years, decades, since I had been in this Mississippi River town. I hadn't been here since Uncle Jake died and Aunt Missy gave me his old brown and white Cadillac (one with long fish tails on the back!), the one he kept in the garage, undriven for years, after his eyesight stopped him from driving.

How quickly those memories returned to me now. The paved road was not paved when I was a child.

Just a dirt and gravel road, but mostly dirt,
        gray Spanish-moss-covered weeping willows
bowing in an unending posture of prayer.
I can remember
        the blueberries and blackberries growing wild.
You could tell which ones I had eaten the most by the color of my tongue.

Just a dirt road ...

and every once in a while you'd see the chickens pecking for food in the yard and then you'd laugh as the biddies and the hens and the rooster scattered when Papa came out to back his big Buick out of the old wood-frame garage.

Papa. I need to tell you about Papa. There is no beginning for me without thinking about Papa. He was a tall, robust, black man. Intelligent, principled, scholarly, a college president—but when he came home, he was just Papa. Papa was my mother's father, and I truly believe I loved him more than anyone. I never heard him raise his voice. He was probably the most even-tempered man I ever knew. When I ran to his office to sit on his lap, I only sat long enough for him to reach for his leather coin purse, take two fingers, and pull out a shiny quarter and give it to me. Papa's quarters never seemed to run out, and off I would go across the campus to buy a Dr. Pepper or a Nehi Grape.

It was a church school called Leland College. It was the training ground for church heroes like Gardner Taylor, J. A. Bacoats, and so many more. Gone now.

Nobody is here now.
Nothing is here now.
Nothing except the freshly paved road.

The buildings are gone. The training school where my sister, Sandra, amazed people that she had already learned to read at age four! Gone.

The dormitories, burned to the ground, not even an ember left to remind us of what used to be. Gone.

And Papa's house, the President's House, the biggest, brightest house with six huge white columns beaming, standing at attention in the hot noonday Louisiana sun. The paved road is there now. The dirt road is gone. Everything, everyone—is gone.

I'm home now. But nobody's here to welcome me. I did what they told me I could do. All the achievements, all the honors, all the everything. I did it; but there's nobody here to tell.

Or is there? Papa is here. Mama is here. Uncle Jake. Aunt Missy. Mama Gladys and Aunt Gladys.

And ol' sharp-dressing Uncle Harold. They are all here.

Not to be seen—to be sensed.

Not to be mourned—to be celebrated.

Celebrated for who they were as persons,

celebrated for what they achieved, even against the odds,

celebrated for what they placed in me,

in Billy, in Sandra, in all of us.

They are here.

I feel their presence.

They are here because I am here, a composite of all that they were, of all that I ever hope to be.

Someone is at home.

These are my beginnings, these characters from my life. You never knew them, but some of each of them is in me. They had a plan for my life from the day of my conception. The plan was a simple one—they gave me to God, who had an even better plan for my life.

So, there I stood, in the place of my beginnings wondering . . . wondering . . .

Have I kept faith with the hope my ancestors had for me?

Am I giving a sufficient return on the investment of time and love they made in me?

Have I placed in my own children the same deposit of love and hope, determination and vision, the thirst for excellence their ancestors placed in me? I hope so.

I do not know how much of my beginnings I can say that I *really* remember. Those things that I do know, however, are significant and critical to who I am and what I will become. I do not know how much anyone can *really* remember about the days of his or her beginning. I do know, without doubt, that returning home is spiritually valuable for all of us. There is a debt to be paid to those who knew us, and loved us, and invested in us before we knew ourselves.

There may be precious little that I truly know. About this, however, there is no doubt: The same God who was with me on the dusty roads of Louisiana still walks with me on the paved streets of urban America. The God who sustained me in the place of my beginning is yet in charge of the place of my ending.

God has not failed me. I must not fail God. I must never forget my human history, my holy history, the history of my beginning.

Because of my history, the people and the God of my history, my soul's been anchored—forever.

Having then gifts differing according to the grace that is given to us, whether prophecy, let us prophesy according to the proportion of faith. . . . Let love be without dissimulation. Abhor that which is evil; cleave to that which is good. Be kindly affectioned one to another with brotherly love; in honor preferring one another.

ROMANS 12:6, 9–10

THE MINISTRY OF UNCLE MUGGA

She really wasn't much to look at, but she was one of the most beautiful people I ever knew. She walked slowly and with a limp. She was just slightly overweight, her shoulders were rounded and stooped, and, as I recall, there were little pockmarks all over her face, but she was beautiful. She lived in a little one-bedroom house down on Washington Street, generously furnished with "early attic" antiques. You always knew without looking that you were in her house from the smell of Clorox, moth balls, Lysol disinfectant, the ever-present Sloan's Lineament, and such.

The really singular thing about this rather unremarkable woman was her remarkable name—Uncle Mugga. Born Myrtle Wills, this is the only woman I knew whom everybody called Uncle, with no hint of the negative; it was rather a misnomer, but it was loaded with respect and love. As children, we called her "Mugga" because we were unable to pronounce her real name—Myrtle. For the life of me, though, I have no earthly idea just why we called her Uncle. (My brother, Billy, says the name came from a church play of some sort and it just stuck!) But that's what we called her. All the kids in the neighborhood, all the kids in Sunday school. Everybody knew her, and everybody loved her—Uncle Mugga.

I'll admit it now. Every once in a while we laughed at Uncle Mugga (behind her back, of course). You have to use your imagination to see Uncle Mugga when she wore her brown cotton stockings (I am convinced she had only one pair!). Trouble was, Uncle Mugga didn't have any support to hold the stockings up; so she would roll them at the top, pull them tight, and then tie a knot in

the stockings just below the knee—garters born of necessity and imagination, I suppose. And according to her, she knew they didn't look good, but they kept her legs warm. Believe me, Uncle Mugga was a scream!

I will venture to suggest that everybody wants a "rich uncle." (I use the term, of course, in its best nonsexist meaning.) You know, the one who considers you the favorite niece or nephew, the uncle who comes visiting, looking for all the world like Santa Claus, bringing presents for everybody; there's always a good time for everyone when your "rich uncle" comes to call. Well, Uncle Mugga was everything but rich in terms of material possessions and wealth. She was as poor as poor could be. She was, however, *our* rich uncle.

How did we reach this dubious conclusion? In order to be rich—really rich—one must learn the lesson of genuine kindness, kindness that is a way of life. Uncle Mugga taught that lesson; her living was anchored in kindness. She would leave her little house and walk down the brick-paved street to our house on Saturday morning and gather us up for a day of fun. It didn't take much to make us happy in those days.

We thought we were really going somewhere when we waited an eternity at the bus stop and rode over to Livingston Park Playground. No Nintendos or Walkmans, CDs, MTVs, or "boom boxes" for us. We were quite happy, thank you, just to swing on the swings, or climb on the monkey bars or jungle-gyms, slide on the sliding board or balance ourselves on teeter-totters. What other happiness could a person want?

Once we were all teeter-tottered out, we'd get back on the bus, going all the way out to Ohio Avenue (probably ten blocks in all!) for a chance to play with "Cookie" and the other kids on the block in the neighborhood where Uncle Mugga's nephew lived. Sometimes she would walk us to the park while we rode our bikes.

But the best was yet to come. She always brought us back and sat us down in her small kitchen and gave us a steaming bowl of homemade chicken noodle soup. It didn't matter—20 degrees in winter (always served with hot cocoa and marshmallows, thank you very much!) or 90 degrees in summer—your day wasn't complete until you had some of Uncle Mugga's chicken soup.

She did all of this because she had her own ministry, "kind-ness." She was not the "nanny" or the baby-sitter. I don't remember ever having such structured child care as she gave us. She just did it because she loved children, because she knew how to make children feel special, and how to make them her own. Simply stated, we were loved. We were never used, we were enjoyed.

I do not know if Uncle Mugga could read or write, but I do know that she loved us far beyond any artificial limitation that she may have had.

Uncle Mugga was faithful. We never had to call and ask her when she was coming. We never had to look for her, she just showed up. We could always depend on her. There was no watch in sight, no clock on the wall, but she was always there and right on time. And she could be counted on for more than taking us to the park. She'd be there to walk us to and from church and to share in silly, childish conversation along the way. And, poor as she was, she always had a coin or two to squeeze into our hot little grimy hands for the Sunday offering plate. You can use your imagination to figure out where that coin showed up—a good bet might be a Nehi Grape.

It's clear to me now that everybody should have an Uncle Mugga. You need an Uncle Mugga in your life to love you just because you are there. Everybody needs an Uncle Mugga who is the living personification of what "extended family" is all about.

It really doesn't take much, this matter of ministry. When you get right down to it, all it takes is a little love, a little kindness, a lot of faithfulness, and a willingness to be kind to someone who really needs it. If you don't understand that, maybe you need to go back and read what Jesus said:

> *And whosoever shall give to drink unto one of these little ones a cup of [chicken soup] only in the name of a disciple, verily I say unto you, [she] shall in no wise lose [her] reward.*

MATTHEW 10:42, AUTHOR'S PARAPHRASE

What a wonderful treat it would be if we could just get back to those times when people were concerned, and cared, and freely gave of themselves faithfully, with no motive greater than kindness. I do not know what long theological terms there may be to explain this faithful kindness. I do not know what hermeneutic there is to unravel the meaning and mysteries of this kind of ministry. I only know that we need more ministers like Uncle Mugga. I only know that we need to return to that time when folk gave of themselves freely, with no hidden agendas or ulterior motives, for no reason other than kindness.

There is no satisfactory way to explain Uncle Mugga's continuous "sermon" on loving-kindness. I wonder if God, in his imagination, *ordained* Uncle Mugga to that rare and marvelous ministry of kindness. Uncle Mugga's ministry was to be the anchor of heart and soul upon which little ones could lean, an immovable anchor of childlike trust. Ah, the imagination of God, who takes time to lay hands on a woman called Uncle.

Oh, how I miss Uncle Mugga! Maybe what the world needs now are those who will abandon the security of the pulpit and the shield of the "call" and the sanctity of the robe and choose instead a Chicken Noodle Soup Ministry.

I never knew how much I needed a hot bowl of Uncle Mugga's chicken noodle soup! By the way, whose Uncle Mugga are you?

Therefore, my beloved brethren, be ye stedfast, unmoveable, always abounding in the work of the Lord, forasmuch as ye know that your labour is not in vain in the Lord.

1 Corinthians 15:58

A CHICKEN WITH ITS HEAD CUT OFF

John Updike[1] was not a remarkable man. In the grand scheme of things, John Updike lived a rather ordinary life. Barely a mention of him was made or a tear shed on the day he died. I remember John Updike in the same way I remember Mrs. Jettie Hooper. We all lived at 603 East Mount Street in Columbus, Ohio. The houses are not there now; even that part of the street is gone, having given way to the coming of U.S. Interstate 70. Jettie Hooper lived to the west of our house and John Updike to the east. There were fences between the yards, but it didn't matter because all the children played behind the houses in Engler Alley anyhow.

My parents were not the only ones to migrate north from the rural south, in the early 1940s. They were a part of what history calls the Great Migration (that is, the Underground Railway, no longer under ground, was clearly visible to all). During this period, many blacks moved from the plantations and tenant farms of the South to the overcrowded tenement jungles of Chicago, Detroit, Cleveland, and the more northern cities beyond. We had come to the Middle West, but our roots, our religion, our relationships, and our hearts were as southern as they could be.

Jettie Hooper's yard, like her home, was always neat and clean, with everything in its place. After all, Jettie Hooper was a deaconess at my father's church (Mount Olivet Baptist), and she lived next door to the Pastor. John Updike, however, was quite another story. John Updike's yard had everything in it from a number 10 tub to pigs and chickens. I do not know how long John Updike had been away from his southern upbringing but it was clear that while he had been transplanted, he had not been transformed. On any given day you could have taken John Updike, his wife, his house, and his yard to any part of the deep South and they would have been quite at home.

For the life of me I cannot remember Mrs. Updike's given name—I think it was Frances. But I do remember that her great skill was making lye soap on the back porch. In fact, she made lye soap for everybody in the neighborhood. Her house smelled of lye soap, she smelled of lye soap, and the yard was always bubbling with her pots of lye soap. That stuff could wash the dirt and the skin right off your body!

John Updike, on the other hand, had a different skill for which he was known. He could truly wring a chicken's neck. Mind you now, even back then he could have gone to the corner grocery store and purchased a chicken already killed, plucked, and dressed (as the old folks used to say); but John Updike preferred the personal touch. He always kept chickens aplenty in his yard. His coops were always full, and chickens were always pecking their way around his yard in search of an errant grain of corn, missed from the last feeding.

I always thought the chickens knew—they had a sixth sense that told them—that John Updike was on the prowl for Sunday dinner. It was always a grand event, with the neighborhood kids hanging over the fences or standing on the porch trying to watch the show. John Updike would grab that chicken by the neck, give it one or two whirls, and, with a forward snapping motion, wring that chicken's neck clean off.

Then it was the biggest mess you've ever seen. The head was gone, but the chicken never knew it was dead. That chicken would run around and flutter across the yard, turning round and round for what seemed a long, long time, then, depleted and drained, it would fall dead. But nobody could beat John Updike at what he did—he was the best chicken-neck wringer in the neighborhood, and everybody knew it.

John Updike's life was perhaps less remarkable than most. He brings to mind, however, that no matter how ordinary we are, and no matter who we are or what we have become, we all bring to any new scene, any new arena, something from our past—we all bring past to present; we can never quite escape what we were before we "arrived." Some come from the places of their rearing and bring with them their lye-soap-making paraphernalia and their chicken-neck-wringing skills and try to hide them, but the remnants of our past are always there in the backyards of our minds and in the closets of our conscience.

Even more to the point, there are those who are so interested in denying who and what they are that they literally spend their lives running around like John Updike's headless chicken—just running around in circles, a chicken with its head cut off. The way we dress, the way we speak, the friends we cultivate can never really erase the real persons God first imagined us to be. For all of our efforts to convince others of what we are, the spectators along the fence of life know what our condition was and what our condition is, and in spite of our frantic running to be and become something we are not, those who are closest to us are aware of the cover-up, aware of the true self that is divorced from the impostors we have become, and in that sense of self-denial we are dead and just don't know it.

I suppose we preachers are really guilty here. There is so much we want to be, so much we need to be, so much that others expect us to be that in the process of simply trying to get Sunday's dinner on the table, we assume too many roles, we try to be in too many places at the same time, we manage to live our lives by multiple agendas and as a consequence we become the proverbial chicken with its head cut off. I know I have done that. I know I do that.

William Shakespeare's Polonius was correct: "This above all: to thine own self be true, and it must follow, as the night the day, thou canst not then be false to any man." How much better to be like the John Updikes of this world—do something well, even if it's just wringing the neck of a chicken. In the process, however, John Updike taught lessons of responsibility, the lesson of caring for one's family even if one must suffer the indignity of providing for one's family while clearly in public view. John Updike did not simply kill chickens for the sake of the process or to be brutal in any way; his was a religion that entailed this simple act always in the context of gratitude for the chickens who laid down their lives that the family might eat. John Updike didn't have much, but he was grateful for what he had. He was not required to kill chickens in the backyard. I suspect he did so simply to keep in touch with the place in life from which he had come.

As with John Updike, how much better it is to be ourselves, to truly confess we are what our past has made of us, and to live with the blessing and the burden of that gift.

ᴍ ake a joyful noise unto the Lᴏʀᴅ, all ye lands. Serve the Lᴏʀᴅ with gladness: come before his presence with singing.

Psᴀʟᴍ 100:1–2

Tʜᴇ ʟᴏsᴛ ᴄʜᴏʀᴅ

*T*here are some values in life that, when lost, are often never recovered. Lost values, lost time, lost love, lost integrity, and lost dreams can slip so swiftly from our grasp. While we make vain efforts to recover, to replace, and to renew, some things we lose are simply lost. The sad reality is that although we are often able to replace "things," what is intrinsic (the essence of spirit and heart), once lost, cannot be replaced and, being lost, often leaves our lives void of hope and joy and meaning.

There is not too much that an average twelve-year-old boy can lose, but then who ever said I was your average twelve-year-old boy? I was a typical P.K. (preacher's kid), full of mischief, full of life and insatiable curiosity. Early on I discovered that I had a gift for singing. Now this is not to say that I had much talent for the intricacies of music, as Marie Carter and the recorded grades at Carter's Music School will attest.

I began my singing in the typical church choir—they called us the Buds of Promise—and Mrs. Bea Willis taught us the music she knew as she affectionately called all of us "Headlong" and "Sweet Potato Head," depending on the mood of the day. Every once in a while I find myself striking out on one of her little ditties:

> *You can make a little heaven upon the earth.*
> *You can drive away the sadness with joy and mirth.*
> *You can help to spread the Gospel of truth and worth.*
> *You can make a little heaven on earth.*

Add to my blossoming musical career the Spring Street YMCA Boys' Choir. Oddly, it was at the YMCA that I learned the beauty of singing a capella and the wondrous treasures of the Negro spirituals. At least I think that's what I learned. Some might suggest that I sang because I was secretly in love with the director, Mrs. Greer. At seven years of age, who cared?

I was barely in junior high school when I heard the announcement on WBNS Radio. The radio station was sponsoring a talent contest and encouraged school-age children to enter for a grand and wonderful prize. They urged, "Please call the radio station today to win the WBNS talent contest!" I did not need to listen to the commercial twice. I was convinced that I had to enter and that I would win—hands down.

My mother and father agreed that I should enter. My sister's best friend, Barbara, agreed to be my accompanist. All I had to do was select the piece I would sing and begin the rehearsals in preparation for my great victory.

I would not choose anything "typical." I wanted a piece that would demonstrate my range, my memory, and my artistic skill, of course. After much discussion, I selected a piece that no one had heard of and that I have never heard since: "The Lost Chord"! Now, I don't know if you're familiar with this piece, but let's just say, "O Sole Mio" it is not.

Rehearsals went well. I had learned the piece quickly. With the talent contest only three days away, I kept thinking, *Bring on the competition!* Problem was, I hadn't counted on catching a cold— a bad summer cold. I took every medicine I could find, insisted that I was fine when asked, refused to cough or sneeze where anyone could hear or see. I was determined to be at WBNS on the right day at the appointed hour. Nevertheless, I was doomed.

The axe fell, as they say. Twenty-four hours before contest time, Mama decided that I would have to withdraw from the competition. I can't remember which emotion I felt first—hurt or anger or both, but I do know that I was mad.

As it usually goes with parents, however, the more I disagreed, the more resolute they became about the validity of their decision. The hour of the contest arrived and departed, and I had not made an appearance. Needless to say, all of my friends had been told about my entering the contest and, needless to say, I lost face with them.

I had lost my opportunity to demonstrate once and for all that I could outsing everybody in town.

And with it I had lost my pride.

I was furious with my parents, and, of course, I recall thinking that I would never forgive them for what they had done.

It was then that I made a decision that I would never forget. I went down to the hall closet and got my yellow rain slicker and the hat that snapped under the chin and prepared to depart. I decided to leave the boots because in July the rain would probably not be too bad.

Then on to the kitchen where I pulled down a jar of peanut butter and, as you might guess, the grape jelly to go along with it. With typical preteenage skill I made three peanut-butter-and-jelly sandwiches, wrapped them in waxed paper and stuffed them down into a brown grocery bag, adding a few bananas in case I needed a snack.

Of course, I wrote a good-bye note and left it on my mother's bedroom dresser:

Dear Mama:

I'm leaving and I'm not coming back.

Love,
Henry

The preacher's kid was running away from home.

I don't recall that I had any money, nor do I remember riding the bus. I do remember that it's very hot in July, especially when you're wearing a rain slicker in 95-degree corn-belt heat. Actually, I guess my run away was actually a walk away.

I had no idea where I was headed, but I did think that I probably needed to travel on some side streets so that nobody would know who I was or what I was doing. It never occurred to me, of course, that half the members in my father's church lived in the same neighborhood, and it's sorta tough to be inconspicuous walking down the street in a yellow rain slicker in 95-degree heat when there's not a cloud in the sky.

When I arrived at the corner of Long and Cleveland, something told me to turn right and go to a street not too far away. It wasn't long before I could smell the peanut butter and jelly, the quickly ripening bananas, stinking like all get-out, all rising up to

discuss the status of my hunger with my stomach. I needed a place to stop and rest.

It was then that I realized I was standing in front of the house of Barbara, my accompanist, who had turned traitor and agreed with my parents. Still, I needed a place to rest, and the porch swing she was sitting on was too inviting to resist.

Barbara was very kind. She never asked about the brown paper bag, and she never asked about the raincoat even though she did suggest that I might want to take it off. Well, time flies when you're resting up from running away and the next thing I knew my mother pulled up in her car and, without a word, waited for me to get in. After a run that must have lasted all of one hour and ten minutes, my Prodigal Son episode was over, the lost had been found.

Now that I am a bit older and just slightly wiser, I know that there are other things that can be lost, things with value far greater than that of my Lost Chord. This cameo out of my life—as revealing as it is humorous—does serve to point to the insanity of running away from anything. In a deeper sense my experience revealed the importance of music in my life . . . and the role music has played in my development and growth.

While I have never wanted to be seen as a musician—the limitations of my musical knowledge have guarded against that error—and I have never wanted to be known as the "singer that preaches," there has always been within me a desire to sing to the glory of God. Singing always seems to put me in another place—at another level, in another dimension. It is the source of joy that the world can't give, so the world can't take it away.

My own congregation will attest that on any given Sunday morning I will strike out on a hymn that is not listed in the morning order of worship. They actually laugh at me (some of them) because they think I'm making these songs up.

> *Lord, I'm running, trying to make a hundred.*
> *Ninety-nine and a half won't do.*

My musicians—arguably the finest in America—are in constant "terror," never knowing just what the song will be, or in what key

I will manage to finally land. They will tell you, these fellow worshipers of mine, that I gain particular joy in singing the songs that
are not in the hymnal, like those songs we sang in Prayer Meeting
down at old Mount Olivet on Main Street.

> *Jesus is mine, Jesus is mine!*
> *Everywhere I go, everywhere I be,*
> *Jesus is mine!*

Who says there's no such thing as Ebonics? I learned even as
a child that such singing provides the context for preaching. Any
church that is authentically African-American would not think of
the preacher rising to preach without the appropriate musical setting.

> *Preach the word, preach the word, preach, preach the word*
> *If I never, ever see you any more.*
> *Preach the word, preach the word, preach the word*
> *I'll meet you on the other shore.*

Oh, I loved to hear the singing of the old hymns of faith ...
common meter, short meter, long meter. These were meter hymns
... hundreds of harmonic sounds that can only come from the
soul, lined and sung to the rhythmical tapping of feet and the clap-
ping of hands. These hymns to God's praise were forged in post-
slavery churches when there were no hymnals, no organs, no
pianos or any musical instruments save the voices of the captive,
unleashed in a concert of freedom. None of those hymns were
ever written down because the whole church learned them by rep-
etition—collectively. And only a few gained the skill to be trusted
by the congregation to line out the hymns of the morning.

> *Father, I stretch my hands to thee,*
> *No other help I know.*
> *If Thou withdraw Thyself from me,*
> *Ah, whither shall I go?*
>
> *Author of faith, to Thee I lift*
> *my longing, weary eyes.*
> *O let me now receive that gift,*
> *My soul without it dies.*

What did Thine only Son endure
before I drew my breath?
What pain, what labor to secure
my soul from endless death?[2]

I suppose the end of my story is that I soon recovered from my running away. In retrospect I can confess that Dear, my mother, was right—my cold really was too bad for singing. Since that time I've been told that Barbara said my rendition of the song was "lost" anyhow, so I was probably spared an even greater embarrassment. Maybe I didn't lose what I thought I had lost, after all.

Now it seems, however, that an entire generation is running away from the music that has soothed our souls, enriched our lives, and nurtured our very being. I fear that in an era so dominated by "praise music," we are in danger of abandoning our songs, the music of our people, the lyrics that, according to Wyatt Tee Walker, speak musically to our own social experiences. We are in danger of losing the chord that for so long has held the soul of our people together.

The songs we sing tell a story—our story. It is, this singing of ours, the opportunity we have to set a melody in the spheres, to sing for ourselves a song that the angels cannot sing.

What's your song?
What's the song you sing when all other voices are silent,
the song you sing when songbirds have hushed,
the song you sing in moments of anxiety and fear when you are literally singing the scared away?

Let no one take away your song.
Let no one silence your singing.
Let no one take away your song—
your willingness to sing.
Sing for your soul—
Sing for your heart—
Sing for your God. Sing!
It's not a contest, but there is a reward.

THE LOST CHORD

Seated one day at the organ
I was weary and ill at ease,
and my fingers wandered idly
over the noisy keys.
I know not what I was playing
or what I was dreaming then,
but I struck one chord of music
like the sound of a great "Amen."

It flooded the crimson twilight
like the close of an angel's psalm.
And it lay on my fevered spirit
with the touch of an infinite calm.
It quieted pain and sorrow
like love overcoming strife.
It seemed the harmonious echo
from a discordant life.

It linked all perplexed meanings
into one perfect peace
and trembled away into silence
as if it were loathe to cease.
I have sought but I seek it vainly,
that one lost chord divine
which came from the soul of the organ
and entered into mine.

It may be that death's bright angel
will speak in that chord again;
it may be that only in heaven
I shall hear that grand "Amen."

SIR ARTHUR SULLIVAN

P.S. Those readers who are of another generation will be pleased to know that as a consequence of a meeting that I held with my father soon after my brief sojourn, I was unable to sit down for quite some time. He taught me a new song!

. . . and ye shall be witnesses unto me both in Jerusalem, and in all Judaea, and in Samaria, and unto the uttermost part of the earth.

ACTS 1:8

GRAHAM CRACKERS, OVALTINE, AND ABSORBINE JR.

Anyone over thirty will readily agree that we gain a greater respect for growing older when the candles on our birthday cake continue to grow to forest-fire proportions. The older we become, however, the greater appreciation we have for the advantages of age.

Tragically, we do not live in a society that values age or aging, nor are we experiencing a generation that does. We see age as a liability. Everyone is still looking for that perpetual Fountain of Youth that Ponce de León was searching for in Florida. Opportunistic entrepreneurs, the creators of those skin-preserving, wrinkle-removing creams and lotions and potions are millionaires many times over. Health spas on every corner are there to remind us that youth is in, old age is out.

Fundamentally, modernity has a genuine, inborn contempt for anything old. Old and beautifully architectured buildings give way to geometric designs of concrete, brass, and glass; old, well traveled, picturesque roads are replaced by superhighways; old landmarks disappear and are reincarnated in the form of strip malls, massive parking lots, and corporate structures; and old truths are lost in an age of relativity simply because, by and large, anything old is usually discarded in preference for the popular and the new. New is in, old is out.

Strange, isn't it, how fascinated we are with the new? Did you ever give any thought to how new is new? Did you ever consider that in order to have anything that is really *new* it would require the creation of this "new" from materials that never before existed? It would literally mandate our making something out of nothing.

Examining this more closely, we come to the conclusion that in order to come up with something totally new one would have to be prepared to live with the liability of having created something so new, so untested, so unexamined that only that person would be able to understand it. This musing leads me to suspect that age is God's way of reminding the formerly youthful how subordinate we are to the things that have gone before.

We would do well to chronicle our spiritual journey—a journey not unlike the weaving of a living tapestry on the framework of a loom designed by those who have gone before. The skein of life-given threads (life's experiences) woven wisely, produce the patterns of personality that make us *us!*

For me, to reject the old in order to embrace the new is a paradigm that is antithetical to the African ancestry from which I have come. Ancestors, those who have lived before us and created the world community in which we now live, are in the African paradigm honored and revered. In a strange but certain way they have not only shown the way, their example continues to live beyond the limitations of their mortality or our own.

Those of us who by birth wear the medallion of blackness, those of us who have been kissed by the African sun and wear her variegated hues upon our flesh, we are the descendants of those who were ripped and torn from African soil, and we must never forget the journey of pain through which our ancestors traveled, nor may we fail to remember the instructional suffering taught by the enslavement of free souls. Those who routinely view African-Americans as Other ought also to remember their own ancestors. None, however, can afford to dwell in the past. All people of faith would do well to realize that God can always—with or in spite of us—do a new thing!

William Hicks (1869–1956), my grandfather, was born shortly after the so-called document of freedom, the Emancipation Proclamation, was signed. Legally, of course, he was not a slave, but he bore within him the painful experience of the life endured by slaves. There was no way that he could fully escape from the painful residuals of this dastardly American institution. Granddaddy knew his name. He knew that the name by which he was called was not his name. He knew that although he was called by the surname of Curtis, it was really the name of the plantation owner from which he had come. So he changed the name from Curtis to Hicks. Just why he chose the latter I will never know. Suffice it to say, Granddaddy wanted a new name, to be a new person, to achieve a new thing.

His was a generation of mandated contradictions: they planted and tilled fields from which they gained no yield; cleaned houses in which they could not sleep; cooked the food they could not eat; and wet-nursed babies they did not birth. My grandfather was told that because he was black he was only three-fifths of a man, worth a mere forty acres and a mule, and forever would be separate and never equal. Living contradictions.

In spite of the pain of oppression, the legal designations, and the social stigma, my grandfather was a preacher. His black hat, his vested suit, his long coat, his slight build, and his keen features separated him from the rest. It was not his physical appearance, however, that was telling. What was distinctive was how he carried himself. There was no question that this man, with his dignified walk and his gentle speech, was an anointed preacher. There was no question that this man was different.

Different—that's the word. Granddaddy was *different.* We never knew when Granddaddy was going to show up. It always seemed to Sandra, Billy, and me that Granddaddy would unceremoniously appear at Union Station in Columbus and we'd be off to gather his trunk and bring him home. And it looked like whenever Granddaddy came, he wound up in my room. When that happened, my room became his room as he just sort of took over because there was no room for anything or anyone else in the room except Granddaddy.

Oh, Granddaddy was different all right. I never knew a day when Granddaddy didn't wear his long johns. From the cold of winter to the dog days of summer, you could always count on the long johns. Add to the long johns the ever-present "jar" that he kept under the bed. You can begin to imagine what we were really up against. Granddaddy was a remarkable and marvelous amalgam of eccentricities, education, high aspirations, noble convictions, and stubbornness. But that's not really what made him different.

Granddaddy's presence was always felt in our home. I can't explain it fully, but even if he never said a word, you knew he was

there. Granddaddy had a lot of aches and pains, and the best rem-
edy he could find was a liberal use of his favorite antiseptic, Dr.
Tischner's, and his tried and tested lineament, Absorbine Jr. I suppose the product has been improved now, but in those days of the
early 1950s Absorbine Jr. must have been the worst-smelling lineament known to mankind. And God help you if he ever asked
you to rub him down. Within twenty-four hours of his arrival my
room would be filled with his steamer trunk, the jar would be sta-
tioned under my bed, my hands would be smelling of lineament,
and our whole house would be lit up with the odor of Absorbine
Jr., a most unforgettable and disagreeable odor.

Granddaddy maintained a running argument with my mother,
affectionately known as "Dear," regarding the use of butter versus
margarine. Granddaddy insisted on pure butter and declared that
no one could pass off margarine for butter on him. Well, Dear took
great delight in using margarine, undetected, whenever she could
get away with it. Granddaddy was different all right, but rarely
could he tell the difference between pure butter and oleo.

Granddaddy knew things that doctors are just beginning to
recognize. He started every day with a cup of hot water. I never
could figure out why anyone would just drink hot water, but he
said it had something to do with his "constitution." It worked.

Then came a cup or two of hot Ovaltine with maybe some
salmon and "buttered" graham crackers on the side. Granddaddy
taught me how to eat graham crackers and drink Ovaltine with
the best of them.

Amazingly, Granddaddy was a man of letters. A college graduate, he was the perpetual student. His writings were published. *A
History of Negro Baptists in Louisiana, Things Necessary for Deacons and
Other Laymen to Know,* and *Nails to Drive* were among them. To hear
him preach was to go to school; every sermon was a teaching
moment. Granddaddy was at least as much teacher as he was
preacher, and he surely was the framed loom upon which my
preaching fabric was woven.

But for all the long johns, the jar, the margarine-and-butter
debate, graham crackers, Ovaltine, and Absorbine Jr., you will
never understand how different my grandfather was until you
understand the pattern of his departures. Just as we never knew

when Granddaddy was coming, we never knew when Grand-daddy was leaving. He would, without warning, come down the steps for breakfast and announce to the family that he had to go off to "save the world." And he meant it.

The world never really had any record of the preaching min-istry of William Hicks. At the time he did not pastor a church, and he had no list of engagements to keep. He was convinced, nonetheless, that his calling was to make a difference, to change a life, literally to "save the world."

By the preaching and the teaching of the Gospel, William Hicks intended to save the world.

With the Bible in one hand, his valise in the other, he was on his way to save the world.

He *imagined* that God could use a lad from the plantations of Louisiana, and so, complete with a brand new name, he forged ahead to achieve the impossible–to save the world.

Maybe Granddaddy was right. I suspect he was. To "save" the world is our calling . . . literally! Those of us who preach now have become far too comfortable with the expectations of the modern pulpit.

We think that the goal now is to remember that Sunday's com-ing and to get the next sermon ready. The goal now is to make sure that we are theologically profound, exegetically accurate, and politically correct. The goal now is to conquer the intricacies of church growth and create megachurches with megapeople, megabudgets, and megamortgages.

Yet the Gospel is not simply good news to make people feel good. The Gospel is the Good News of salvation through Jesus Christ. Jesus said it, and my Grandfather believed it:

> *Go ye therefore, and teach all nations, baptizing them in the name of the Father, and of the Son, and of the Holy Ghost: Teaching them to observe all things whatsoever I have commanded you: and lo, I am with you alway, even unto the end of the world.*

MATTHEW 28:19–20

No matter how different we are, the goal ought to be the same: to be energized enough to leave the comfort of the pulpit and pew and move out to the world—to save the world. My grandfather taught it, my father lived it, I believe it, and now one of my sons has the same calling on his life—save the world, save the world, save the world! Nothing less will do.

Now I have yet to acquire an affinity for Granddaddy's Absorbine Jr., but to this day there's a bottle of Ovaltine and some graham crackers in the kitchen pantry. My wife, Liz, likes butter, and I like margarine. (And I can tell the difference—sometimes!) There's no "jar" under the bed, but we're still leaving room for Granddaddy's next unexpected visit. It almost seems as if we're just sort of expecting that any day now Granddaddy will just show up!

When I call to remembrance the unfeigned faith that is in thee, which dwelt first in thy grandmother Lois, and thy mother Eunice; and I am persuaded that in thee also. Wherefore I put thee in remembrance that thou stir up the gift of God, which is in thee by the putting on of my hands.

2 TIMOTHY 1:5–6

"A CREDIT TO THE RACE"

Funny, isn't it, how things stick in your mind? For years a thought may leave you and then, without warning, there it is again as fresh as the day you first heard it. When I think upon it, however, I suppose my greatest training was "thought training"—training that came through those expressions, the colloquialisms that taught more than I knew. My mother was best at this. She had a thousand of them. Here are a few:

"Never look a gift horse in the mouth."
"There's many a slip twixt the cup and the lip."
"If you make your bed hard, you have to lie in it."
"A soft head makes a hard behind."
"Take it easy, greasy; you've got a long way to slide."

In every sense of the word I am a child of the forties—a period of time when our nation was embattled in World War II; FDR allayed the nation's fears with his "fireside chats"; Eleanor Roosevelt demonstrated civil rights in action; civil rights were asleep in an undiscovered cocoon; and Mary McLeod Bethune headed up the so-called Kitchen Kabinet. A remarkable period—the forties—and I am a product of that time.

As a consequence of these significant socio-political realities, my perceptions of the world and my understanding of who I was and my awareness of my limitless potential of becoming took form and were shaped, molded, and refined.

I do not claim total recall of all the lessons taught and learned early on but I do remember with all the clarity of yesterday the monumental mandate to be "a credit to the race." Day in and day out my parents and the adults with whom I came into contact constantly gave a clarion call for all of us to be *"a credit to the race."*

I remember a day in my life when I had more aunts and uncles than I could count. They were the marvelous love connection rooted somewhere in the once-upon-a-time so familiar to my soul, never to be forgotten. I remember a day gone by—"once when we were colored"[3]—when we knew who we were—in spite of . . .; when we knew that we had something precious to uphold. According to the textbooks, we were poor, but we never knew it! Others were more materially advantaged than we, but we never recognized it; others had more reasons to be happy, to celebrate, and yet we seemed to have happiness every day. Our mothers or our grandmothers or our aunties saw to it that we went to school with clothes clean, hair combed and neatly parted, our shoes shined, our bellies comfortably filled, and our faces greased down with absolutely no trace of "ash" (if you don't know what that is, don't ask!).

We knew what it was to be the first family to have a television on Mound Street, and the whole neighborhood would gather with us to see Ezzard Charles, Jersey Joe Walcott, and Sugar Ray Robinson fight for the "title" (really fighting for the race) on the *Wednesday Night Gillette Cavalcade of Stars.*

> *To look sharp—and be on the ball,*
> *To feel sharp—every time you call,*
> *To stay sharp—use Gillette Blue Blades*
> *for the quickest, slickest, shave of all!*

It all had something to do with being "a credit to the race."

Being a credit to the race had to do with a sense of pride in who we were and what we were accomplishing as a people.

Being a credit to the race held no implication of proving ourselves or impressing others.

Being a credit to the race meant that the "Negro" had something worth nurturing, maintaining, upholding.

Being a credit to the race did not suggest that we had something to defend; it meant that collectively we have something to be proud of.

Being a credit to the race encouraged and applauded personal achievement, but the joy of the accomplishment was shared by the people as a whole. Perhaps we could not be presidents of corporations, perhaps we could not be leaders of industry, perhaps some of us could not read or write, but, no matter, we could still be a credit to the race.

It seems so simple now. It wouldn't seem much in 1990s terms, but in 1940s terms *any* certificate earned, *any* diploma awarded, *any* degree achieved was a "credit to the race."

Securing a job downtown that made a briefcase a part of your work attire was a credit to the race. Being the "first Negro" to achieve some status or climb to some pinnacle, to navigate uncharted waters that heretofore had been reserved for those of the majority culture was what it meant to be a credit to the race. Going to college, achieving against the odds, and, in spite of the opposition, doing something positive and productive that would benefit the race was not an option. It was neither an alternative nor an accident. It was an expectation, a requirement of your birthright of blackness. My father told me more than once that I would be black for the rest of my life and I was expected to be "a credit to the race."

Whatever happened? Here I am at the close of the century watching my wide-screen TV and all I can see is violence in the streets, our young boys wearing their pants below their "belt lines," our young girls willing to wear anything at all as long as it's "the bomb!," our jails bursting with black men, and more black men in prison than we have in colleges. All the while the world pays more attention to an ex–football player in California who can't get his story straight, a basketball player in Chicago who can't decide what psychedelic color God intended for his hair to be, and a gifted young golfer–son of an African-American man and an Asian woman–who is unclear about the identity he desires to claim. Whatever happened to being "a credit to the race"?

Perhaps my problem is that I was born in the wrong year, at the wrong moment in history. My expectations are rooted in history. In the days of my youth, my heroes were A. Philip Randolph and Mary McLeod Bethune, Roy Wilkins and Whitney Young,

Marian Anderson and Thurgood Marshall, Jesse Owens, Jackie Robinson, and Ralph Bunche. They were my heroes and my heroines because somebody told me that because of who they were and what they had accomplished on my behalf, each had become a credit to the race. Somehow knowing who they were let me know who I was and what I could also become. I knew that I, too, could become a credit to the race.

What have we done that has caused us to forget the sacrifice of so many? The year was 1972 when I first visited Western Africa. In the nation of Ghana—formerly the Gold Coast—I discovered the remains of slave castles, those places where Africans were held in cages until the slave ships could come and take them through the Middle Passage to these shores. As I stood there in that castle I wanted to feel the confinement, the painful confinement of that small cubicle. So, I crouched and twisted my body to fit in one of those tiny spaces just to connect flesh and soul to that of my ancestors so many, many years ago. And I did.

Once there in that unimaginably tiny space, I wondered how we could forget the sacrifice of so many. What have we done—or not done—that has caused us to forget the sacrifice they made, the journey they took? How did we arrive from the nations of Western Africa and then permit our children to forget how we made the journey? How did we come all the way from the great palaces of Africa where we reigned as kings and queens? How could we forget the loving, extended, spiritually grounded, hard-working families from which we have come to this point where our behavior and the behavior of our children blatantly belies and denies our regal heritage? Or, from the reverse vantage point, if our lineage was not royal, our ancestors still provided for us a history and a heritage of which we can be proud. How could we ever forget such a legacy?

Imagine what life would be if only we would recapture, individually and collectively, the notion of being "a credit to the race." Imagine what pride our children and our children's children would know if only they could learn the joy of making a contribution to something larger and greater than themselves. Imagine what a difference it would make if our children not only knew whence they came but, more important, where they are headed.

Ours is a day of blended families and blended cultures. Yet I remain old-fashioned enough to insist that we can never blend away the reality of our heritage and our blackness, we can never blend away who we really are. Ours is a challenge to liberate our children to the knowledge that they need not be frozen by social or biological identity and that their blackness is their heritage, and maturity of character is their goal. Ours is a mandate to assure that our children are not ashamed to achieve, to strive for excellence in what they do and in who they are.

Perhaps my imagination is not yours, but is it imagination to long for the day when we are no longer ashamed to insist that our children stand on the high ground of excellence and achievement? This is not a time to lower our standards, this is a time to raise our standards. This is not a time to excuse our behavior by the tragedies of slavery and segregation, nor is it appropriate to point to the inequities of public education as a justification for permitting what is common among us. This is a time to rise above our limitations and set our sights on those things the world believes are beyond us. It is not simply in the imagination of God but in the intentional will of God that a new generation of children rise up with a new agenda of purpose and priority that will honor the sacrifice of ancestors gone before and pave the way for progeny yet to come.

Fleecy locks and dark complexion
cannot forfeit nature's claim;
skin may differ but affection
dwells in black and white the same.

Were I so tall as to reach the pole
or to grasp the ocean at a span,
I must be measured by my soul
for the mind is the standard of the man.

AUTHOR UNKNOWN

PART *Two*

IMAGINE
THE FAITH

While the concerns of my life are rooted in the past, they are matured in the present. Only now have I come to a more complete appreciation of the ideas and concepts that were taught by those who were central to the formation of my faith. As I look back upon the roots of my faith, I realize that most of the preachers I heard and the Sunday school teachers from whom I learned were often unlettered and unsophisticated in terms of theological concepts or critical biblical scholarship. Yet, I confess that the lessons that have been most lasting were taught by some who could not read their names. Their lack of learning was fully compensated by an intense and intimate relationship with the God of whom they spoke and with whom they talked. When they taught, they used phrases and expressions that have lasted through the waste of years. When they spoke of the Jesus whom they had come to know, they spoke of him as a "Rocking Chair," a "Lawyer," or a "Doctor." These saints of the church of my childhood perhaps unknowingly used the parabolic method of Jesus—to speak of the ordinary, common events and circumstances, and from their essence to extract lessons of living. They used these phrases to express verbally that which they experienced spiritually and emotionally. These are the phrases that come only from an imagination kissed by the Eternal, and they have become anchors for my life.

My little children, these things write I unto you, that ye sin not. And if any man sin, we have an advocate with the Father, Jesus Christ the righteous: And he is the propitiation for our sins: and not for ours only, but also for the sins of the whole world.

1 JOHN 2:1–2

A LAWYER WHO HAS *NEVER* LOST A CASE!

I slipped quietly into the last row of pews in Superior Court. The crowd I had expected failed to appear. It was a case of murder. A black man accused of killing a black woman. There was no question of guilt or innocence, only a question of how severe the penalty would be. Now they were here because of the verdict of a black jury, and the sentence would be handed down by a black judge. No need for a crowd, really. Just another case of Black ... on Black ... on Black. An old, old story. Rehearsed too often, repeated too soon.

I had come for the sentencing today at the request of a broken father and a distraught mother. Their son, their only son, was tried and convicted—a life sentence now hanging over his head. They needed spiritual support. I was there to offer whatever I had. In reality, there was little I could do. Testimony had already been given. Neither my presence nor my words could prevent the judge from following the letter of the law in so obvious a crime. With nothing to offer, I was content to sit nearby in an attitude of prayer for both the innocent, the guilty, and the dead.

He looked the part. Brooks Brothers suit, wing-tip shoes, silk tie. Conservative dress with just a touch of class. Obviously, the attorney for the defense. I watched him closely ... wanted to hear his every word. What does an attorney say when the verdict has been given, the case is closed, and only sentencing remains? An appeal to the facts would no longer be appropriate. An appeal to the law would be unnecessary. What more could be said to protect the guilty from the punishment deserved?

If ever I look back on my life and wonder what there was that I should have done but failed to do, it was to become a lawyer. I have no doubt about my call to the Christian ministry, but I also have no doubt that there's a lawyer in me trying to get out. Sometimes in the days when I permit myself to think of things undone, I can still see myself standing before a judge and jury pleading someone's hopeless case.

Criminal Law—nothing else would do for me. The more difficult the crime, the better. Give me the friendless, the most wretched, the most despised. Let me speak for those who have no voice. Let me argue for those who have nothing and no one on their side. Let me be the one to stand between one life and ultimate destruction and death. Thurgood Marshall, Charles Hamilton Houston, Kenneth Mundy, Herbert Reid, and all the rest would find in me an apt pupil. Somewhere, I know, there's a lawyer in me.

I expected more from the defense when it came time to speak of final sentencing to the judge. (I chided myself that I really have been watching too much *Perry Mason*. On the other hand, I know good legal work when I see it. Unfortunately, on this day I was not seeing it.) I really expected at least a feeble attempt at some grand argument—even a contrived grand argument—to lessen the blow of the inevitable weight of judgment and the law. It was as though the attorney for the defense had given up before he began. Soft-spoken, muted tones, no urgency or energy. Presentencing guidelines in place, all that was left was to go through the motions. It was all so matter-of-fact. Nobody really seemed to care. After all, real lives were at stake here. And I saw the young man slump in his seat,
    hope gone,
        essentially defenseless,
            no one really to plead his case.

And there I sat. Just a preacher. Not a lawyer. What on earth could I say?

Then I remembered that all these years, going in and out of church, if the old folk in church taught me anything at all it was that

Jesus is a Lawyer who has *never* lost a case!

I don't know where they got that phrase. I suppose I thought they just made it up. But over the years, it has become, I suppose, one of the clichés of the faith. It has become, no doubt, a kind of mantra or shibboleth for the African-American Church. The more you say it, the more the tones of its incantation are heard, the more the chant is intoned, the more you expect it to occur, the more you come to understand that even this old worn-out cliché is not only a part of the *imagination* of God, but also an anchor of faith for a people who have themselves been in such a defenseless posture. How odd of God to express his imagination with such pedestrian language. Can one take such imagination seriously?

Never lost a case?

> *And, behold, a certain **lawyer** stood up, and tempted him, saying, Master, what shall I do to inherit eternal life? He said unto him, What is written in the law? How readest thou?*
>
> LUKE 10:25–26

> *But when the Pharisees had heard that he had put the Sadducees to silence, they were gathered together. Then one of them, which was a **lawyer**, asked him a question, tempting him, and saying, Master, which is the great commandment in the law?*
>
> MATTHEW 22:34–36

> *Then answered one of the **lawyers**, and said unto him, Master, thus saying thou reproachest us also. And he said, Woe unto you also, ye lawyers! For ye lade men with burdens grievous to be borne, and ye yourselves touch not the burdens with one of your fingers.*
>
> LUKE 11:45–46

Jesus always seemed to run into conflict with the law and with lawyers. But we are told that he is a lawyer who has *never* lost a case.

Truth be known, one never appreciates a lawyer until one needs a lawyer. I do not value a lawyer until

I can no longer speak for myself ...
I am accused and cannot deny it ...
I am innocent and cannot prove it ...
I am guilty and cannot escape it ...
I am wronged and I need to expose it ...

Not until it appears that
my arrest is imminent;
my indictment is sealed;
my adversaries are lined up to testify against me, and
I can hear the cold clang of steel shutting me off
and taking the fresh air of freedom from me.
Then I know I need a lawyer ... a good lawyer ...
a lawyer who has never lost a case.

I watched as they placed the handcuffs on him, in full view for everyone to see. His face turned toward the floor, unable to look in the direction of his family, tears flowing. Father standing stoically against this ill wind, seeking to be strength for mother now bent over with such incredible pain, such unassuageable grief.

In how many other courtrooms is this pitiful scene replayed? How many lives are destroyed? How many black males, in the prime of life, will be crammed into human warehouses, shut off in their most productive and reproductive years?

What's that? I hear slaves singing:

That awful day will surely come
the appointed hour make haste;
when I must stand before the bar
and stand the solemn test![1]

And what about me? When will my day come? How can I sit in the courtroom of another's sentencing and not realize that in some respect I might sit under the same condemnation. I cannot imagine it. Neither can I *imagine* all the things God has planned for me. I only know that I must be open enough to face the reality of my humanity, to acknowledge that there is some crime, some sin of which I am guilty and for which I might well stand before judge and jury. I cannot escape the question: When will I be forced to stand in some unknown court, before some unknown jury, some unknown judge and hear the sentence in my case?

There will be no question of my guilt. A good lawyer would tell me to admit nothing. Still, like David,

"I acknowledge my transgressions:
and my sin is ever before me."[2]

The evidence is clear and plain for all to see:
". . . though your sins be as scarlet . . .
    though they be red like crimson . . . !"[3]

I have a Lawyer.

My Lawyer must be victorious.

My Lawyer will be victorious because my Lawyer is the Son of the Judge.

My Lawyer will be victorious because my Lawyer is a court-appointed Lawyer, appointed by the Judge to be my Advocate.

My Lawyer will be victorious because the plan for my pardon began in the heart of the Judge.

I recommend my Lawyer.

If you want a lawyer, if you need a lawyer, remember that this Lawyer will not defend on the grounds of justice. Neither you nor I could stand justice!

This Lawyer will not defend by some technicality of the law. He will not claim that you were not given your Miranda Rights. He will acknowledge your guilt and tell the Court that you were "shapen in iniquity and in sin did [your] mother conceive [you]."[4]

This Lawyer will not defend you by seeking to plea bargain for lesser punishment for a lesser crime.

The defense for your case and mine is *mercy!* Nothing but *mercy!* I heard old Deacons pray, "Now, Lord, mercy suits our case!" I don't know how our ancestors knew it. They had no sophisticated biblical knowledge. They studied no doctrine or theology or exegesis or hermeneutics. But they knew something about Jesus, they knew something about this Lawyer who never lost a case, and John left this word for you:

> *My dear children, I write this to you so that you will not sin. But if anybody does sin, we have one who speaks to the Father in our defense—Jesus Christ, the Righteous One. He is the atoning sacrifice for our sins, and not only for ours but also for the sins of the whole world.*

1 JOHN 2:1–2 NIV

Jesus—my Lawyer! Your Lawyer! Our Lawyer!

A Lawyer who has *never lost a case!*

Wherefore seeing we also are compassed about with so great a cloud of witnesses, let us lay aside every weight, and the sin which doth so easily beset us, and let us run with patience the race that is set before us, Looking unto Jesus the author and finisher of our faith.

HEBREWS 12:1–2

MY ROCKIN' CHAIR, MY WALKIN' CANE, MY LEANIN' POST!

There are few pleasures of the ministry like that of the rural pastorate. If I had my way, a good stint in a country church would be a prerequisite to any other form of ministry. A country church, unlike any other, teaches love, kindness, humility, poverty, patience, and a brand of theology the likes of which they won't teach you at Harvard Divinity School or any other theological seminary.

The day I walked through the doors of the church on George Street I had absolutely no idea of what to expect. Still in seminary, with my gorgeous new bride at my side, I had been given an opportunity to pastor what many called a "starter" church. Among those who "started" in this little country church was the late Mordecai Johnson, later to become President of Howard University in Washington, D. C.

Membership? Only seventy members if they all showed up on Easter Sunday.

Budget? Don't ask.

When you looked at it, the church looked like a Currier & Ives postcard. A white clapboard church complete with a hip roof and with a tiny stream gurgling and bubbling through the backyard. No need for a key to the church. Door's open, just go right in. If you get lost coming through town, just turn right at the one and only flashing yellow light. Welcome to Second Baptist.

One thing about it. The folk knew how to love you. And you had no choice but to love them in return.

What's not to love?

Lucy Jackson—

best fried chicken, corn pudding, and collard greens this side of heaven.

Pauline Carter—

tall, robust, husky voice, but she could stir up some home-made rolls that would make angels envious.

Ethel Banks—

self-appointed historian of the world. Kept everything—every book, every document, every scrap of paper known to man—all in the living room of her house!

Horace Shelton—

spent his time instructing me on the difference between a car and an automobile. Literally translated, what he meant was that anything I drove was a car. Anything Horace drove was an automobile.

John Poles—

Who could forget John Poles? I will never forget the night I was conducting my very first church meeting. John Poles arrived just off from his security job. He came into church wearing his pistol on his hip. The meeting recessed.

"Brother Poles, meet me in the kitchen, if you please, Sir!"

These were the special souls, the sweet spirits that made Second Baptist the wonderful church it was. They nurtured Liz and me, just starting out in marriage and in ministry. They became our family. This was a family that could only be born in the imagination of God.

The problem at Second Baptist was that the members were all related to each other, every last living one of them. You never knew to whose aunt, uncle, or cousin you were talking. But everything you wanted to learn about pastoring a church you could learn right there—Second Baptist Church on George Street.

They warned me about Mother Jackson. Two weeks before I met her, one of the family members decided I needed to know about the notorious Mother Jackson. She was the "mother" of the church, in every sense of the word. Nothing happened at Second Baptist without Mother Jackson's approval. And preachers lived or died depending on what Mother Jackson thought of them.

Rumor had it that early on Mother Jackson would slap the preacher as a means of asserting her authority. (I never thought there was any truth to the rumor.) We met one Sunday morning in the small vestibule of the church.

"Pastor, I'd like to introduce you to Mother Jackson."

"Very well. Good day, Madam!"

"Good day!"

I did not bow. She did not bend. I would come to appreciate in years to come that Mother Jackson was not just the "mother of the church," she was everybody's mother. In her own way, she drew us in, loved and protected us so that we never had to fear her wrath or the wrath of any other. Something special happened that day in the vestibule that endured for ten years until, nearly ninety years old, I tenderly laid her to rest.

Truth be known, Mother Jackson was a sweetheart.

Set in her ways. Yes.

Old-timey. She had a right to be.

Loved the Lord. Without question.

A preacher's friend. None better.

Every Sunday morning Mother Jackson and Pauline would have a pound of bacon and a dozen fresh eggs on my desk. To this day, my wife is the most creative egg cooker known to man.

You really need to meet Mother Jackson. An octogenarian with spirit and verve others many years her junior have yet to achieve. She walked with a cane, more for balance than for any physical limitation, I suspect. Then, too, she had a right to a cane. Over her years she had reared more than twenty foster children in her home. No wonder everybody in town called her Mother.

Her home was an antique lover's dream. Exquisitely furnished, the minute you walked through the door you knew you were in the presence of a woman of substance.

Over in the corner of Mother Jackson's living room I spotted a wooden rocking chair. I didn't just spot the chair, I was captured and captivated by it. Just imagine its rounded arms supported by thirty-eight spindles, its ornate, fanned back, a marvelous mixture of curved and straight lines. This chair, made of the finest cherry wood, had, like its owner, borne the weight of many years. You just knew that with its gentle rocking motion, many problems had been solved, many anxious hearts quieted, many sobs hushed, and many tears dried. In Mother Jackson's living room I found a chair you could depend on. The comfort of the chair was in its design and detail. No need for cushions or pads, its comfort was in its presence and not in its pretense. I'm not usually one for antiques, but this one I loved.

Every Sunday you can hear somebody claim that Jesus is like that. How do they say it?

"He's my rocking chair . . . my walking cane . . . my leaning post."

That's what we need. A rocking chair, a dependable rocking chair, a place to rock your cares away. That's what we need. A walking cane, something to steady our footsteps and give strength to feeble hands. That's what we need, you and I, a leaning post, something that will hold steady and will not move. We need a post on which to rest when the storms of life are raging. We need a post on which to lean, in the cool of the evening, and hold a conversation with a friend, while the children chase fireflies in the night.

Not very sophisticated is it, this talk of rocking chairs, and walking canes, and leaning posts? The imagery would never make its way into weighty theological works or in volumes of religious philosophy. No. In order to understand what our parents meant by these words you have to use your imagination.

You have to be tired enough to appreciate an old wooden rocker in the living room or on the front porch, right next to the creaking wooden swing.

You have to be vulnerable enough to know that you can't always rely on yourself, you can't rely on the strength or energy you used to have. You need something stronger, something greater, something that won't bend or break. You must acknowledge the presence of the unseen forces that take strength from your own limbs—arthritis and bursitis and all the other "Itis brothers"—to be unable, sometimes, to put one foot before the other. You must know the pain in your joints that insults you with its presence even before you put your feet on the floor.

You have to be open enough, and free enough, to enjoy the pleasure of resting on a post, not caring what the world says about you. You must be willing to lean on the post when nobody else comes down the road to lean with you. You must be secure enough to hold a conversation with the post, telling it all your troubles, confiding all of your hurts, confident that the post will not move, that it will be there on all your tomorrows. You must be certain that the post won't tell your secrets, no matter how dark or grim they may be. When you live in a world where nothing is dependable, nothing is secure, nothing is stable, nothing will securely hold you, and everything will let you down, it's comforting to say with utmost assurance:

Jesus is my Rocking Chair ... my Walking Cane ... my Leaning Post.

She was on her deathbed. Only a few hours and Mother Jackson would make her final flight. With the breath left in her body she told Pauline and the rest: "Take the rocker. Save it for Pastor Hicks and Liz. It belongs to them!"

It's in our living room now ... Mother Jackson's old rocking chair. It's old—we've had it repaired once or twice—and it still creaks. It has a broken spindle or two. Yet there remains a lot of love in that chair. A lot of faith. A lot of trust. Thanks be to God for the blessing of our rocking chairs. I just believe that God ordained something as simple as a rocking chair to provide the support, the strength, and the comfort we need at times and places we could never imagine. The imagination of God provides for us life's little treasure—a God-blessed, Spirit-kissed rocking chair. I thank God for rockers, for canes, and for leaning posts, and most especially for all the Mother Jacksons in our lives.

And now, every once in a while, we just pass by and for no reason at all we sit in that chair. We honor Mother Jackson. We honor her memory. And every time I see it, I remember that

Jesus is my rocking chair!

There was a man sent from God, whose name was John. The same came for a witness, to bear witness of the Light, that all men through him might believe. He was not that Light, but was sent to bear witness of that Light. That was the true Light, which lighteth every man that cometh into the world.

JOHN 1:6–9

MY LIGHT IN DARK PLACES

Miss Bertha used to scare the life out of us. Every evening, just before bedtime, all the kids—Sandra, Joyce (my mother's sister), and I, along with any other neighborhood kids who hadn't gone home yet—would gather around Miss Bertha's bed to hear her one and only bedtime story:

> Mai oui, Mai oui, I'm at your door.
> Mai oui, Mai oui, I'm in your hall.
> Mai oui, Mai oui, I'm by your bed.
> Mai oui, Mai oui, I'm at your head.
> I Gotcha![5]

Every night. We heard the same story every night. We knew how it would begin and how it would end. We knew the identity of the culprit, and we rejoiced that the culprit would give the time for such delightful terror. We didn't know at what point it would end, and we never knew which one of us would be touched by the wonderful hands of Miss Bertha.

As far as I can remember, Miss Bertha was my step-great-grandmother. Don't ask me how it happened. Just take my word for it. The most wonderful attributes about Miss Bertha were her hands . . . and her legs . . . and her arms . . . and her fingers. Every limb was grotesquely twisted and gnarled by crippling arthritis.

She could never hold us,
she could only touch us.

But her touch was the special gift from a very special love.

I never knew a day when Miss Bertha fed herself or drank a cup of water unassisted. Never saw a day when Miss Bertha got up, dressed herself in her Sunday-go-to-meetin' clothes, or marched off to church with everybody else. Come to think of it, I never remember a day when Miss Bertha was not in the front bedroom, propped up on a special pillow, holding out a ready smile for all her children who made a beeline to her bedside. Mamma Gladys, my grandmother, saw to it that Miss Bertha was always fresh as sunshine.

And Miss Bertha (step-great-grandmother "griot") always had a story to tell. If it wasn't her night-time rendition of "Mai Oui," it was her attention-getting noonday telling of "Johnny, Get Your Gun!" part storytelling, part singing, pure imagination.

Now, in order to understand what I'm saying you must use your imagination. Mai Oui was a game played best when the lights were out and everyone was hot and sweaty with the Louisiana heat.

In later years, Mama and Daddy would play this silly game, after we were all tucked in, scaring us half out of our wits. Strangely enough, I have no idea what Mai Oui means. I am confident that it is spelled phonetically, and I can only guess that it has its rootage in some of the French Creole voodoo customs prevalent in bayou country (Louisiana) during those years. The game was played with the lights out, the floors creaking, wind shadows dancing, the other kids screaming in unison—yet all you could hear and feel was your own breath heaving and your own heart pounding. My friend, this was fun!

Do you sleep with a night light on? Be honest. Just down the hall, is there a night light or a light in the closet in the other bedroom? I have my own special night light. In part, I need the illumination should an unexpected walk to my daughter's room down the hall be necessary, but I suppose you could say that I have returned to those years when I expected good ol' Mai Oui to jump out from nowhere and do I don't know what all. Maybe you didn't call your midnight visitor Mai Oui. Maybe you're more familiar with the "bogeyman." No matter, all of us are acquainted (whether we admit it or not) with these imaginary, demonic, satanic apparitions of darkness that rob us of our sleep and make us curators of the night.

Journeying with me down the pathways of my life, you will find that my life was not and is not composed of continuous sunshine. Nor is yours. You will find that my life has been filled with its share of nights, of unrelieved darkness. Life's alternating currents take us from sunlight to midnight and back again.

And in those moments when the night comes . . .
    and there are no friends to be found
when the night comes . . .
    and your head is "bowed beneath your knees"
when the night comes . . .
    and the tranquillity of your home is disturbed . . .
    the state of your health is suddenly imbalanced . . .
    your future is grim and your fortune has slipped
        through your fingers . . .
    your ship has come in with no cargo on board,
when the night is upon you
    and it is "blacker than a hundred midnights
    down in a cypress swamp,"
you and I need . . .
in that moment . . .
a night light, a light in dark places.

Perhaps in the record of my spiritual journey, I should never make this entry: "If the truth be known, I need a night light. I cannot escape the night, I need a night light." The prophet Isaiah said, "The morning cometh, and also the night" (Isaiah 21:12). There is certainty in the coming of the night.

If my morning comes, my night is not far behind.
If my success arrives, some failure is close on its heels.
If my assets are in order, my liabilities will soon overtake them.
I need a light.
    I need *the* Light,
        a night light.
Where is the night light?
    The Light for my stumbling feet,
    the Light-guide for my tortured path,
    the Light that will permit me to see the way
        when there is no way?

Hold back the night!
Hold back the night!
I'll be alright,
If you hold back the night.[6]

Our ancestors, yours and mine, were much smarter than are
we. They knew that their survival and that of generations to come
would depend on the availability of a night light. That's why they
said so often, "Jesus is a Light in Dark Places."

It takes imagination to put yourself in the hold of a slave ship
setting sail from Africa to America, to smell the stench-filled darkness of the night, and to sense the reality of death, your traveling
partner. Dark Places.

It takes imagination, courage, and faith to seek the peaceful-
ness of sleep on the dirt floor of a slave cabin, separated from family and kin, and to hear the screams of brutality, and to be a
witness to a holocaust of blackness for which the world has never
shed one tear. Dark Places.

It takes imagination to endure and live with hope while impris-
oned in an urban dwelling, seeking the elusive blessing of sleep,
where death walks the streets, stalking the accused and the innocent, where semiautomatic weapons make mockery of law and
order, and where it is unnecessary to wait for three strikes to be
"out"! Dark Places.

Yet it takes no imagination at all to know that, far too often,
Mai Oui is not simply a childish game, and for far too many the
bogeyman is the parent or the priest, the mentor or the minister,
the trusted or the emulated, who became the source of our fright
rather than the wellspring of our hope.

I cannot escape the reality—nor do I wish to—that I cannot
endure the anxiety of the darkness of this world without a light.
What is needed is more than a night light: *The Light.* I thank God
that there is a Light:

And the city had no need of the sun,
neither of the moon, to shine in it:
for the glory of God did lighten it,
and the Lamb is the light thereof.

REVELATION 21:23

*In the beginning was the Word, and the Word was with God, and
the Word was God. . . . In him was life; and the life was the light of
men. And the light shineth in darkness. . . .*

JOHN 1:1, 4–5

Miss Bertha taught me an awful lot about the night. She taught
all of us that the "night," the imposed darkness, can be endured
and we need never utter a cross word, never complain, never fret.

The night cannot be avoided but it can be endured. It can be
endured with grace, with dignity, with hope, and with a smile.

Miss Bertha endured the long nights of her suffering and pain,
not because there was something redemptive in the experience,
but because of a faith that held her close throughout the nights.
Miss Bertha endured the nights, and we can endure the nights, not
because of our faith in faith, but because the One who is the center of our faith holds you . . . and me.

Those of us who played and prayed at Miss Bertha's bed saw
that her whole life was radiated by a light whose source many have
never found. She frightened us with her silly words but, in the
same motion, she literally loved our "scared" away.

My children—Henry, Ivan, and Kristin—all know the story of
the infamous Mai Oui. I told them the story not just to scare them
but to ensure their connection with a part of my heritage that is
rightfully their own. My greatest prayer is not that they will know
Mai Oui but that they, and their children, and their children's children will know the One who is The Light in Dark Places.

God imagines that we will need a Light in Dark Places. How
odd of God to prepare a Light, to send a Light so we will not be
left to stumble in the dark. Because of God's love, angels hover
near to bear us up on their wings.

Thank God for the night.

Thank God for those lonely places,

    those vulnerable places,

        those places where we must trust in God

           and in God alone.

I imagine that Miss Bertha's legacy to me is that when arthritis steals the activity of my limbs, I will have her grace to touch

someone's life with a love and with a childlike humor that will scare the night away.

There is One who is the Light. There is One who is the Night Light!

Weeping may endure for a night, but joy cometh in the morning!

PSALM 30:5

> *After this there was a feast of the Jews; and Jesus went up to Jerusalem. Now there is at Jerusalem by the sheep market a pool, which is called in the Hebrew tongue Bethesda, having five porches. In these lay a great multitude of impotent folk, of blind, halt, withered, waiting for the moving of the water.*
>
> JOHN 5:1–3

MY HELP WHEN I'M HELPLESS

The apostle John tells us a story about a man who had a life membership at the "Bethesda Spa and Health Club." Some aggressive salesman had sold him one of those "special deal" memberships, the kind that winds up costing you twice as much as you originally thought you had agreed to. Anyway, Bethesda had a great spa. The whirlpool was especially nice. Marble flooring in the pool. Flowing natural water. Natural juices. Natural light. Natural air. Natural everything. This place was an ecological, environmental, physical-fitness, health-and-wholeness, get-your-body-back-in-order paradise! Just what the man in the story needed.

I suppose John wouldn't have bothered to tell this story were it not for the fact that the man in question had the longest continuous membership of anybody in the history of the club. This man had been a member for thirty-eight years. One would expect that after thirty-eight years this man would be a specimen of perfect physical health. His biceps and triceps and quadriceps and all the rest would be the envy of every other member of the club by now. Every muscle in his body would be trimmed and toned to a "fare-thee-well!" No annual fees for this guy; by now he had stock in the place.

You and I know, however, that this was not the case. The man at Bethesda Spa and Health Club was as pitiful a person as you've ever seen. After all these years his body was frail, his limbs atrophied, his joints now swollen masses of pain. His friends had told him how therapeutic the whirlpool bath would be. It would be especially beneficial because rumor had it that on special occasions something miraculous seemed to stir the water. Crippled (read: physically challenged) people were known to go into the water broken and come out of the water completely whole.

He had been there for thirty-eight years. A dues paying, card carrying, lifetime member of the Bethesda Spa and Health Club. Can you imagine it? After all these years, however, he was still in pain, unable, as he said, to get into the pool for the "stirring" of the water. It is not long then, as the story goes, before Jesus speaks to this pool-side paralytic and says to him, "Take up your bed and walk!"

One of the most engaging commercials on television in recent years involved the old woman who is lying helpless on the floor, looking up with the most pitiful eyes, saying:

"Help! I've fallen and I can't get up!"

The commercial is designed, of course, for persons who may need to call for special emergency assistance and who may be unable to do so because of some very special physical limitation. The item to be sold promises to summon a friend or the Emergency Medical Service unit simply at the movement of a finger. No need to say a word; just press a button, and help is on the way. Critics would probably say that the commercial is a technical disaster at best (or an overstated claim, at least), but there is no question that it gets the message across. Inwardly, all of us fear that day when, like the woman in the commercial, we are down, defenseless and helpless. We imagine the words in our own mouths: "Help! I've fallen and I can't get up!"

I do not know the woman in the commercial. I assume she was an actress, paid for her performance. Still, she cut close to the fabric of the human predicament. For you and me, it is not simply that we have fallen and are prey to some accidental circumstance over which we have no control. Imagine what it means to be helpless, to struggle day after day knowing that there is no help. Everything is available to us and within finger-tip reach, and we could be better, except for the fact that we have no help. To be helpless is an assault to the ego, one's self-esteem, until at last we see ourselves as less than we ought to be, less than we should be, less than we want to be, simply because we have no help.

Do you know what it's like to help someone who is really helpless? No? Let me tell you one of my experiences. During my college days one of my summer jobs, believe it or not, was driving an ambulance. I found out, first hand, what it was like to go into the home of suffering, pain, and grieving and not to simply offer help, but to *be* help. Perhaps you have never had this experience, but imagine, just for a moment, the anxiety of weaving through traffic, running traffic lights, racing to respond to a call for help because you know that every second counts. Imagine the hurried movements in some still midnight when you are yet able to hear the cry for human help even above the chilling, screaming wail of a siren.

Driving home the other evening, trying to hit the erase button on the activities of the day, it all came back to me. I saw the familiar flashing lights and a car pulled alongside an electric pole by the road. Without a Good Samaritan instinct to my name, I moved quickly past the scene until an inner voice said, *Go Back!* A quick U-turn in the road, and in a moment I had returned. Cautiously I approached the two-seater sports car, and I could see that it was not by the pole, it was wrapped around the pole. The frigid air accentuated the steam now billowing from the engine and I was horrified to see that the steering column had been forced to the passenger side of the car. A head twisted to the side, an arm limply hanging, one person conscious, the other unconscious. I heard the cry, "Help, mister, help us!" I did not know them, they still do not know me. Yet in the canyon of my mind I hear the echo still, "Help, mister, help us!" In a moment, the flash of lights, the piercing siren screaming in the night, a helicopter hovered, paramedics running. Help was on the way.

Maybe that's all we need to know. Help is on the way. Whether your helplessness involves an emergency summons of an ambulance before dawn's early light; or if yours is permanent residence in a place of healing where nothing seems to work, nothing seems to cure; or if your lot is to be down and out on the road of life, with no one nearby to hear or to care; or if it is an aloneness, a friendless solitary existence, the message for this day is that help is on the way. For you. Especially for you.

Interestingly enough, when we are faced with the kind of circumstance those two persons in the wrecked automobile faced, we call it an "accident." By definition, an accident is an unforeseen, unexpected occurrence, usually unpleasant, that results in some injury or loss. I have come to learn, however, that those things we call "accidents" are, in reality, "*Godcidents*." Godcidents are those events that come into our lives that provide a platform for God's work in us and for us. Godcidents are never capricious. They are part of the intentional will of God; they are the events that gain our attention and refocus our minds. Godcidents shake us, but they also shape us; they deny us, but they do not destroy us; they open to us a new avenue of relationship, a nurturing dependence that reminds us that while we are in our fallen state God is always present to lift us up and once again stand us on our feet.

By the way, the woman on the floor in that commercial has a message you probably didn't hear. The little device she uses has a button to push to summon help. It's battery-operated, and the button doesn't work unless it stays connected to the source of its power. There are moments, I suspect, when each of us has fallen and in those moments we are quick to reach for the spiritual resources of faith and prayer to lift us from our state. The truth in every case is, however, that we are never rescued, we are never lifted, we are never saved, unless we are connected to the Source of ultimate power.

There's a plant, a tree, in the room where I'm sitting. At least that's what it looks like to me. One day I'll get my wife to tell me the precise botanical name for this oversized plant. It has wide leaves; in fact, the leaves look like the leaves on an ear of corn. A dracaena something or other. At any rate the tree is leaning at about a thirty-three-degree angle, and I believe I've discovered why. The tree is too tall for the height of the ceiling, and this has forced it into an unnatural position, but, more important, it has bent toward the sunlight streaming through the sliding glass door nearby. Looks like the dracaena knows the secret. There is help, there is a power source, if we but lean to the light.

By the way, if you're down and can't get up, or if you are at the Bethesda Spa and Health Club and it still does no good, or if you are counted as an accident, a mere statistic on some lonely road of life, never give up. Remember Jim Valvano, coach of the North Carolina State basketball team, who suffered from incurable cancer. His words of encouragement:

"Don't give up. Don't ever give up!"

I will lift up mine eyes unto the hills, from whence cometh my help.
My help cometh from the Lord, which made heaven and earth!

PSALM 121:1–2

Imagine it. Help is on the way!

Then they went out to see what was done; and came to Jesus, and found the man, out of whom the devils were departed, sitting at the feet of Jesus, clothed, and in his right mind: and they were afraid.

LUKE 8:35

MY CLOTHES WHEN I'M NAKED

Stand in any authentically African-American church on any Sunday morning and I guarantee you, before you leave you will hear these words: "He's my clothes when I'm naked, my shoes on my feet...."

I wonder what all that really means. After hearing the words so often, we find they have nearly lost their meaning. Or have they?

The classroom was filled to capacity. We were only a few sessions into the introductory course in Old Testament, but we knew that something special always took place in this class. We were only first-year seminarians but we knew, when we stood in the presence of someone who had been anointed, that very soon our heads would be blessed by that same oil. There was always an air of expectant tension whenever James Alvin Sanders spoke.

I do not know just where Dr. Sanders was that morning, probably in some intricate detail of textual criticism or some other obscure matter of biblical interpretation, but his lecture was disturbed by the raising of a lone hand. The unabashed student had only one question:

"Dr. Sanders, when will you make all of this relevant?"

Silence. The class sucked its collective breath. We could not believe he had asked the question. Before an eminent Old Testament scholar, a translator of the 151st Psalm,[7] and an interpreter of the Dead Sea Scrolls, no less, and someone dares to raise the issue of relevance.

We will never forget the day that student was offered up on the altar of sacrifice. Departing from his prepared lecture, Dr. Sanders proceeded to give us all a magnificent lecture on the relevance of the Old Testament, a theme that was to endure through-out the rest of the semester. There yet remains the echo of Dr. Sanders's lectures: "Let God be God," or "The Old Testament is as biblical as the New," or his constant refrain, "He who walked in Eden now walks in Galilee." Still, in classic manner, Dr. Sanders offered what was at least an erudite expression of compassion and an affirmation of the question, while at the same time it was a stern rejoinder to an ill-timed and ill-advised question.

To be honest, that question of relevance has haunted and hounded me for all the years of my ministry. Karl Barth suggested years ago that every preacher ought to climb the stairs of the pulpit with the Bible in one hand and the newspaper in the other. The task of the ministry is not to make the Bible relevant but to reveal that relevance so that others may see.

Church folk can be so stuffy.

So sanctified.

So pious and pretentious.

Who cares about the church games we play?

> The claims we make?

> The songs we sing?

> The sermons we preach?

Who cares if there is no Good News in our gospel?

We must not be lulled to sleep by the harmonies of hymns the world will not sing. Our majestic cathedrals will crumble into dust,

> our extensive, high-tech, computerized organizations

>> will pull apart at the seams,

>>> and no one will ever know that something called the church passed this way if we are not concerned about this question of relevance.

It *really* is a question of relevance.

There is no doubt in my mind that there are persons within the congregation I pastor who have no idea why I do the things I do. The endless struggle to organize, to program, to preach, to teach, to evangelize, to witness . . . it never ends. These poor people are doing something in church every day. They come to church on Sunday and leave on Tuesday. The kingdom must be coming . . . tomorrow!

Here's the clue. Every anointed ministry worthy of the name must find means and method to answer the question, When will you make this relevant?

The question of relevance.

When people are lost, the only thing they need is direction. That's relevant.

The homeless require shelter.

The sick require a physician.

The hungry require food.

The naked require clothing.

Nothing else will help. Nothing else will do. Nothing else is relevant.

If in the twenty-first century the Christian church lives, it will live because it has discovered the secret of relevance. The secret of relevance, I suspect, is found in imagination.

The city had never known heat of this magnitude. For weeks the temperature hovered at the 100-degree mark; 95 degrees was considered a cold snap. And this was the week I decided to hold a revival—a tent revival, outside, in the heat, for seven days.

For thirty years I have presided over revivals:

Preaching to the saved.

Singing for the sanctified.

Trying to reconvert the converted.

It's not working. We might as well be honest and confess; it's not working. All those traditional, "safe" things that church folk do won't work anymore. We're preaching—nobody's listening. It's time to be relevant.

It takes some imagination to see the mammoth white tent rising from an inner-city school yard. Just think of it—a 129-year-old established institution abandoning the comfort of its padded pews, carpeted floors, and air conditioning all for the privilege of holding services in a hot and steaming tent! A hundred and fifty voices singing. A thousand wooden seats on bare ground.

Night after night they came.

We fed them.

By the hundreds.

The hungry, the homeless, the hopeless.

By week's end over six thousand came!

Literally, they came for the Bread of Heaven.

They came to eat.

They remained to hear the Gospel; either out of courtesy, gratitude, or need ... but they remained and heard the Gospel.

I know another preacher, a long, long time ago, who used this method with far greater success:

> *Philip, whence shall we buy bread, that these may eat?...*
>
> *Philip answered him, Two hundred pennyworth of bread is not sufficient for them, that every one of them may take a little....*
>
> *Andrew ... saith unto him, There is a lad here, which hath five barley loaves and two small fishes....*
>
> *And Jesus took the loaves; and when he had given thanks, he distributed to the disciples, and the disciples to them that were set down, and likewise of the fishes as much as they would.*
>
> JOHN 6:5, 7–9, 11

Jesus understood that there is a relationship between bread and belief. Life, like bread, must be broken and in the breaking it is blessed. Jesus understood what it was to make religion *relevant!*

The text was typical for a summer revival: Luke 15. Even the homeless had heard this sermon more times than they cared to remember. There had to be a way to make Luke 15 breathe, to resurrect an old story in a way that would bring new life.

Some years ago I traveled to Hong Kong. One of my prize purchases from that trip was a silk-and-satin brocade robe. A great robe. I loved the way it felt on my shoulders. Made me feel regal when I wore it. I must be somebody!

Luke 15.

Prodigal son.

Fatted calf.

Ring.

Robe.

As the sermon came to its end, I extended the opportunity for men and women to accept Christ. Many came to be received into the arms of the body of Christ. I noticed one among them—a young lad. Simply to look at him you knew he was homeless, that his life had been hard, his struggle had been long.

The prodigal son was standing before my very eyes.

I talked to him. Directly to him.

I told him that no matter how far away he had been, and no matter what he had done, and no matter what the circumstances of his life, the Father had commissioned me to welcome him home. I say again,

If in the twenty-first century the Christian church lives, it will live because it has discovered the secret of relevance. The secret of relevance, I suspect, is found in imagination.

The robe. Give me the robe. My Hong Kong, silk-and-satin brocade robe. I took the robe, placed it on his shoulders, and welcomed him to his Father's house.

Theatrical? Yes. Disingenuous? No.

I knew this: This man probably couldn't spell *prodigal*. No doubt he was not acquainted with fine silks from the Orient. He did know, however, what it was like to live in an urban pigpen, to sleep where others would never rest, and to eat what others had thrown away.

I knew this: The church would be irrelevant, the Gospel would be irrelevant, preaching would be irrelevant, Jesus would be irrelevant unless Jesus, quite literally, is able to clothe me when I'm naked!

You had to see him walk. You had to see him walking down the street when the revival lights were dimmed and most of the people had already gone home. You had to see his head thrown back, shoulders straight, stomach pulled in, self-esteem restored, self-worth renewed. You had to see him walking down the street in a silk-and-satin brocade robe in 100-degree heat. In that moment his stomach was full, his soul was saved, he had clothes on his back, a prodigal came home on the wind of imagination.

And the son said unto him, Father, I have sinned against heaven, and in thy sight, and am no more worthy to be called thy son. But the father said to his servants, Bring forth the best robe, and put it on him; and put a ring on his hand, and shoes on his feet: And bring hither the fatted calf, and kill it; and let us eat, and be merry: For this my son was dead, and is alive again; he was lost, and is found. And they began to be merry.

LUKE 15:21–24

When in some personal, private moment, you think about what all of this has to do with you, it will require no imagination at all to realize that all of us are naked. Job reminds us that at our beginning and at our end we are naked (Job 1:21). How many are the circumstances of our lives that expose us and make us vulnerable, naked. Before our secret sins, naked. Despite the pretensions of person or profession, naked.

Still, there is One who accepts us as we are, naked and incomplete. There is One whose love will clothe and shield us from the vagaries of life. There is One who, in peculiar yet imaginative ways, brings relevance to our church and relevance to our world. That One is God, who comes and who is able to clothe, to cover, and to change. Whether in pigsty or in palace, there is One who is able to clothe us when we are naked.

Your robe is waiting!

A WAY OUT OF NO WAY

Because of its theme of liberation and freedom, the Exodus narratives are central to the heart and spirit of the African-American church. The parallel experience of slavery, the process of systematic dehumanization, the incredible struggle for escape, and the constant search for security in a hostile land are the core concepts that make this story our own.

The thread that holds the entire narrative together is the miraculous work of God. It is not simply that God moves in an unexpected way. Rather, he moves in a way that cannot be explained or understood: Things happen that should not happen, events occur for which there is not one credible shred of reliable testimony to justify them. In the midst of nothing, God does something. God just does what God does—and that's that!

Sometimes I think my children think I'm not listening, but I really am. Most parents usually are sometimes busy, sometimes distracted—but always listening.

Henry, my eldest son, whom we affectionately call Speedy, was always an inquisitive child. I used to complain that Speedy never saw a button or a knob that he didn't like. Ivan always talked about preachers; Kristin still wants to hear music at its highest decibel; but five seconds after climbing into the car, Speedy would examine every knob and button within sight, never managing of course to put the radio back to the frequency where he found it.

In his own way a thoughtful lad, Speedy rarely asked penetrating questions, but when he did you could be sure he would have a good one. We were driving to church one day when out of the blue Speedy asked, "Why do you always say Jesus is a way out of no way? And sometimes you say that Jesus opens doors that no man can shut. Why do you say that? It just doesn't make sense to me."

I'm sure I answered the question, but I still remember how thoughtful the question was for a lad so young, and I've never been quite certain that I answered the question as fully as I might have. The years that have come and gone since his question are many, but I always wanted to find a way to give a more direct and meaningful answer that he could understand. Finally, by the Spirit's marvelous prompting, he called one night and without knowing gave the answer to the question himself.

I spent the last three years of my college career as a student on the campus of the University of Arkansas at Pine Bluff, then known as Arkansas AM&N, one of the original land grant colleges. While there, I put my Bea Willis musical training to good use and managed to receive a full scholarship as a bass vocalist in the Vesper Choir, directed by Professor Shelton McGee. It was not a large choir, but it was an excellent choir. The voices, most of which came deep from within the rural communities of the State of Arkansas (places like Altheimer, Dumas, and Forest City), were pure and fresh. We were young, gifted, and black.

At that time AM&N was not a part of the State University system. As a consequence our dormitories were overcrowded, classrooms outworn, textbooks outdated, and every building in need of serious repair. It is a testament to the seriously in-grown faculty that the school produced more than her fair share of teachers, lawyers, doctors, and scientists. Because the school was a step-child of the state, never receiving the support or the resources of the University of Arkansas at Fayetteville, the president was always in a crunch, always begging the state legislature for financial assistance.

The state legislature met periodically in Little Rock, the state capital. At the time of appropriations, Dr. Lawrence A. Davis, or "Prexy" as we called him, always wanted to put his best foot forward. We were called on to travel in a school bus to Little Rock, there to perform for the legislators, there to literally sing for our supper. The year was 1962 (or was it '63?) when we made our annual visit. We were to sing at a local hotel. Of course, even then we were ushered in through the back doors, though they said we didn't have to be.

Speedy called the other night. Speedy is now a graduate of Morehouse College and the University of North Carolina. He is an executive with NationsBank in Charlotte, North Carolina. We are proud of his accomplishments.

"Daddy."

"How are you, son?"

"I'm fine. How's Mom?"

"She's great. Where are you anyhow?"

"I'm in Little Rock, Arkansas."

"Oh, really? And where are you staying?"

"I'm staying at the hotel in downtown Little Rock."

I could not believe my ears. It's been at least thirty-four years since I first visited that hotel ... through the back door. And now my son, my firstborn, is stretched out in a king-size bed in the same hotel (it's been remodeled now and given a new name) in downtown Little Rock. By the way, he checked in with his Gold American Express Corporate Credit Card. I don't think he's ever been to the little college down the road where his mother and father met and went to school, and now he's there to do business for one of the largest banking corporations in the world. And, by the way, he didn't have to sing.

Soon our children come to the places we have been. Soon our children come to experiences in life that were kept from us because of the color of our skin and the time in which we were born. Our children must never be permitted to forget the sacrifice, the pain, and the shame that others have endured in order that they might be where they are. I cannot nor should I attempt to live out my life through my children's achievements, but I must confess that I am certainly pleased and proud that NationsBank sent my son for one trip to Little Rock, Arkansas. It was a vindication for which I have long waited.

Those legislators who made us sing for a pittance—at the time they were still serving ham hocks and neck bones in the school cafeteria—never knew when or how or if I would return to the place of such great humiliation. But I did return and in a larger, stronger variety. My son—H. Beecher Hicks III—went through the front door of that hotel all because God made a way out of no way. God opened a door that no man can shut! When the door opened, I imagine God smiled.

PART *Three*

IMAGINE
THE CHURCH

*W*hen you have been in the church all your life, it's hard to imagine what life would be like without it. I am among a generation that was nurtured, if not born, between the pews of the church. While our children are entertained by characters on a television screen or ideas that flash from the Internet, we learned of life from real humans who literally gave flesh and blood to the church.

There are no characters like the people you will meet in a church. Whether you need romance, tragedy, melodrama, or comic relief, take a seat on a pew and watch the real world pass by. Only God could imagine some of the people whom I have met in the church and whose lives have affected my own. These are people who, despite their failures, their faults, or their idiosyncrasies, sustained the church, created institutions of higher learning, formed the organism that would birth the civil rights movement in America, and prepared all who came within her walls for the living of a positive life beyond cynicism, doubt, and despair.

You have never met these friends of mine, but if you read on you will discover that you know every one.

And as they were eating, Jesus took bread, and blessed it, and brake it, and gave it to the disciples, and said, Take, eat; this is my body. And he took the cup, and gave thanks, and gave it to them, saying, Drink ye all of it; For this is my blood of the new testament, which is shed for many for the remission of sins. . . . And when they had sung an hymn, they went out into the mount of Olives.

MATTHEW 26:26–28, 30

COMMUNION

*D*id you ever notice how words tend to take on meaning far beyond their original intent? After years of usage, sometimes words themselves seem to take on lives of their own. Perhaps that's why you can look at the cold definition of a word and the definition itself never seems to measure up to the reality (or realities) the word was meant to convey.

Did you ever think about the word *Communion*? Look at it again. It's a funny-looking word. Old Noah Webster has it right in between *commune* above and *Communist Party* below. The proper definition, of course is

> *the act of sharing one's thoughts,*

or

> *a group of Christians professing the same faith
> and practicing the same rites,*

or

> *sharing, celebrating the Eucharist, or Holy Communion.*

Adequate definitions all, I suppose. My experience of communion, however, runs far broader, far deeper.

First of all, you must understand that we did not have Sunday afternoon football. Oh, I suspect some teams were playing football somewhere on Sunday afternoon, but if they were we had no television sets on which to watch it. Sunday, in my early years, was not a day to be entertained by twenty-two men beating the dickens out of each other for fun and profit. On Sunday afternoon we were always in church. (Aren't you supposed to be in church on

Sunday afternoon?) And on the *first* Sunday of the month we were always there for what we now call The Lord's Supper. Most often, however, we simply called it Communion.

Now you must understand that, unlike its place in contemporary worship, Communion was never sandwiched in between the offering and the announcements. Nor was it tacked on as a necessary but worrisome appendage at the end of the service. No. Communion was special, worthy of a service all its own. Some churches called it Covenant Meeting because the Church Covenant was always recited and reaffirmed at every such gathering. It took me years to understand why the preacher (my daddy!) always read the Covenant one line at a time, with the people repeating his words. I now know that many could not read but were drawn closer to the fellowship through this simple act of sharing. That's special.

It was in this service that the new converts in Christ were taken to be baptized. The baptismal pool was hidden just below the pulpit and the kids would gather around before the service to watch the deacons take up the floor and fill the pool. The water was always something less than pure: you could always count on stray splinters of wood or bugs floating in the water, and, summer or winter, it was always ice cold. The first Communion was at the water where lives were brought, and washed, and changed.

Communion was special for us because of the testimonies one would hear. Oh, the phrases of our faith, especially when we testify:

> "I said I wasn't gonna tell nobody,
> but I just can't keep it to myself...!"

> "... and I want you to pray for me, church,
> those of you who know the worth of prayer!"

> "... a' please pray my strenk [strength] in the Lord,
> that I be the one that he be calling for
> in these last and evil days ...
> for these is perilous times!"

You could count on them. Usually we knew who was going to testify and when they would testify, and we knew most of what they were going to say.

If they didn't say it, of course, they would sing it. You just had to be there to hear old Sister Upchurch light up the church, singing:

When you see me runnin' I got Jesus on my mind,
When you see me runnin' I got Jesus on my mind,
When you see me runnin' I got Jesus on my mind,
   I got Jesus on my mind!

He did not know one note from the next, but Deacon Wheeler could start heads swaying and feet pattin' when he began singing, "Shine on Me! Shine on Me! Let the Light from the Lighthouse shine on me!"

Oh, they had hymn books. But the songs they really liked to sing were not written, they were transmitted from one generation to another. Meter hymns. Dr. Watts' hymns, my daddy called them. No drums. No bass. No synthesizer. No Hammond. Just old "Bea" Willis, a converted honky-tonk piano player, who knew precious little about the fine intricacies of classical music, but who knew how to make a piano move, knew how to love the song out of you, and never missed a note on the way. I can see her now, with her head thrown back, a little cocked to the side, with that high-pitched laugh: "Hee, hee! Sing, children!" And before you knew it, the church would be in an uproar.

Communion *meant* something then. The deaconesses took special pride in laundering the cloth and napkins for the Lord's table. No laundromat for these linens.

They washed,
   and stretched,
   and starched,
   and ironed them by hand,
every fold, every crease in its place.

It took time. It took a sense of pride. It took love. It made Communion special.

And strange things could happen in Communion.

Turn on your imagination! There we were, one first Sunday afternoon, not an empty seat in the church. The choir loft was filled to capacity, and the service at the Lord's table had just begun. It was one of those quiet moments, when everything is still and every eye drawn to the flicker of candles. Then all eyes were closed in a moment of personal, meditative prayer.

BAM!

Without warning one of the long bombard pipes from the old pipe organ toppled over and fell across three rows of the choir. Dust flying. Sopranos squealing. Altos running. Basses ducking. You never saw such a mess in church! Fortunately, no one was hurt and no one really cared about the old wind pipe organ anyway. Nobody could play it except Katherine McGill, and she played it only on those Sundays when the senior choir sang one of those anthems they didn't really know how to sing. But God knows they tried.

It wasn't long after that that it was Daisy Hammock's time. Now Daisy was something special in and of herself. First of all, Daisy had a song. And nobody could sing it the way she could. The thing was she walked when she sang, and every step accentuated every note ... or was it the other way around? No matter. You get the point. Is your imagination turned on?

When she walked, she walked sideways. You know, left over right. When she walked, she sort of used her hip to point the way, and in between she threw her head around so you knew she really meant what she was singing:

> *I have a dear Savior, I do, don't you?*
> *I live by his favor, I do, don't you?*
> *I want him to bless me, to hold and confess me,*
> > *completely possess me ...*
> *I do, don't you?*

By the time we got to Daisy's part in the service we were really in high gear. Most of the time, though, Daisy waited to sing her song when all the deacons and deaconesses were standing around the church prepared to lead the congregation in the eating and drinking of the elements.

Well, sir, the pipe organ wasn't enough. Daisy's singing wasn't enough. She decided, bread and wine in hand, that this would be just a wonderful time to be overcome with the Spirit and do her little shout. Trouble is, it's hard to shout with a little glass of Welch's Grape Juice in your hand. But Daisy started shouting and grape juice started flying, bread crumbs were on the floor everywhere, purple polka dots jumped on those white starched deaconess dresses, and no one knows to this day just how that service really ended.

We children laughed at it all then. Those strange events of worship amused us no end. But now I know that in every sense of the word it was Communion. Those years permitted us to share in ways that we have not shared since. Somehow, through it all, we really managed a Communion that transcended Webster's definition or any other for that matter. Communion then meant

sharing common experiences,

remembering the hurt, rejoicing in the triumph.

We did not laugh *at* each other,

we laughed *with* each other.

And we knew that Sister Upchurch *really* was doing the best she could, and that Deacon Wheeler *really* did believe in that lighthouse. And we knew that even Daisy had her own brand of sincerity, if often misunderstood.

I guess the point of it all is that in real Communion (a sacrament of life rather than liturgy) you can really be yourself. There on Sunday afternoon we could be ourselves because the falling pipes were indicative of the facets of our lives—social as well as political and economic—that things were falling all around us. And who cared if somebody took a little strut across the front of the church? Everybody in there had a little strut in them, and Daisy just showed us how to do it.

Soon—one day soon—the church will reclaim this freedom. We will commune not as a matter of form but as a unique Christian fellowship that finds strength in the presence of one another and, in so doing, finds liberty.

We will come to understand that church and community must not be separate.

We will find unity in Christ as we find unity in the common experiences of our lives.

We will come together and, in so doing, find union.

Union in ourselves.
Union with each other.
Union with our Christ.
Communion with Christ.
I want to know that kind of church. I want to be a part of that liberated and liberating kind of church.
I do.
Don't you?

When Jesus came into the coasts of Caesarea Philippi, he asked his disciples, saying, Whom do men say that I the Son of Man am? . . . And Simon Peter answered and said, Thou art the Christ, the Son of the living God. And Jesus answered and said unto him, Blessed art thou, Simon Barjona: for flesh and blood hath not revealed it unto thee, but my Father which is in heaven. And I say also unto thee, That thou art Peter, and upon this rock I will build my church; and the gates of hell shall not prevail against it.

MATTHEW 16:13, 16–18

PASS THE NEWSPAPER, PLEASE

All four of us had piled into our brand new Oldsmobile and prepared ourselves for the long trip south. Our journey was tinged with the mixed emotions of excitement and sadness. We were sad to leave Pittsburgh, a church and people we had grown to love, but we were excited about the possibilities of new ministry in the Antioch Church, an old and historic congregation in downtown Houston. Our departure had been somewhat traumatic as there was real pain in the separation from Mount Ararat. So much had been accomplished in less than five years, but now, by God's guiding hands, we were moving on.

Houston greeted us with its sunshine, and soon we had moved into our new home. All we had to do now was to grow grass in Houston's sandy soil and all would be well. Or so it seemed.

Antioch was, and yet remains, a proud church—the oldest African-American Baptist Church in the city. It was the pulpit of several distinguished pastors who had moved on to even greater ministries. To this century-old institution came an energetic, albeit brash young preacher with more ideas than patience and with a determination not to relive history but to contribute to and to make history.

My secretary, I discovered, was an institution within the church who took meticulous care with the affairs of the church. The staff consisted of a secretary and a janitor and a preacher. The building was in disrepair, with a portion of it sinking into the ground because of Houston's classic erosion problem. The baptismal pool was inoperable; no one could really remember the last baptism that had taken place here. And the music, let's just say it was an interesting blend of uninspiring music. Add to the mixture a young preacher still new at the craft, and you had a combination that only heaven could bless. Yet there were wonderful people there who were serious about the church and who welcomed us with open arms.

It was not long, however, before I found myself in direct conflict with the established "pillars" of the church—descendants of the church's founder, keepers of the traditions and curators of the church's ecclesiastical antiquities. Besides this, an insipid lethargy and inertia within most of the congregation did not bode well for the change that I believed was necessary for the continuance and survival of the church. I would quickly learn that there were those who intended for Antioch to remain just as she was. Little did I know how forcefully they would maintain their position or how willing they were to sacrifice everything in order to do so.

In such an environment it is easy for a preacher to learn to lose faith—to lose faith in his ability to breathe life into the church organism and to lose faith in the people who are the church. How tragic the lot of the preacher/pastor who, when called upon to complete a task, finds the roads blocked, the tools removed, and the resources insufficient.

When one is exposed to persons who deliberately sabotage programs and plans, when one is subjected to those who object to ministry for the sake of objection and yet is called to preach the Gospel to those who have no good will for his ministry, one comes extremely close to hate. I do not care to remember the number of ruptured church meetings and conflict-filled board meetings over which I have presided. I do not know how many times I have driven the long road home uncertain and unsure if there was any reason for continuing, any reason for preaching, any reason for continuing this ecclesiastical charade.

Strangely enough, it was in this maelstrom of conflict that I learned some of my greatest lessons in ministry as well as some of my greatest lessons in life.

I discovered in my pilgrimage with this people that it is often difficult to preach in a negative environment. Many were the days when it appeared that my words were hollow, that there was not a receptive climate or soil in which the Word could take root, be nurtured, and grow. Sunday worship was often perfunctory. We followed the order of worship, but it was often hard for the Holy Spirit to gain a breakthrough. Either I had been sent to God's Alcatraz or John's Patmos, or I was certainly standing in the middle of Ezekiel's Valley of Dry Bones. In order to survive this situation I would need either John's vision or Ezekiel's wind. This could not remain the same; it would have to change mightily or it would only get worse.

I was surprised one Sunday morning to see that the church was relatively full. The worship was going well, the Spirit was high. This was a morning when I thought I had a powerful sermon, and I was eager, ready to preach. Midway through the introduction to the sermon I saw something I had never seen in church before or since. Two women whose names I do not recall had taken their seats on the very back row on either side of the center aisle. One of them, I noticed, had brought along her copy of the Sunday morning *Houston Post*. While I struggled to proclaim the Gospel, what to my wondering eyes should appear but the front page section (or was it the comics?) being handed across the aisle. Throughout the entire sermon these two women were actually reading and sharing the newspaper while I preached.

It took some years, but I have come to terms with this disruptive and disrespectful behavior. I have come to view their activity not only as a request for attention but as a statement of their need for love. They wanted my attention, but they did not want me to love them as I loved the rest of the congregation; they wanted a special love that recognized who they were and what they had to offer.

I have also come to realize that it is because of this hostile and alien environment that the Gospel is so necessary and so relevant. These were not persons who had no need for the Gospel—they were shouting as loudly as they could that they needed Good News, acceptance, love, forgiveness, and reconciliation now more than ever. If Moses could preach to murmuring children in the wilderness, if Ezekiel could "open the doors of the church" in the middle of a cemetery, if John the Revelator could preach to churches whose candlestick had been removed and whose places of worship had become the very synagogue of Satan, why not I?

Harold S. Kushner in his book *How Good Do We Have to Be?* addresses the issue of sibling rivalry as revealed in the book of Genesis.[1] Kushner points out that in every case of sibling rivalry, brother against brother (sister against sister), the Genesis account ultimately comes to the point of sibling reconciliation:

> *Isaac and Ishmael come together at the grave of their father, Abraham. Jacob and Esau overcome their memories of past hurts and fears and fall into each other's arms after twenty years of estrangement. And in the greatest story ever written about brothers overcoming hatred and jealousy, Joseph is reunited with the brothers who sold him into slavery. . . . When he finally had the power to [get even] . . . Joseph discovered that he didn't really want revenge. He wanted family. And he couldn't have family unless both sides transcended the hatred and hurt feelings of their growing-up years.[2]*

I have discovered that in that church and in most churches there is a long period when pastor and people go through—and grow through—their "growing-up years." Our maturity comes only through the passage of years when hurts are able to heal and when the things over which we were so conflicted seem to pale in their significance. There are far too many weightier issues, pain that must be eased, tears that must be dried, the issues of life and death that are before the ministry and before the church, and these cannot be overrun by pettiness either in the pulpit or in the pew. We do ourselves a disservice when we fail to permit the persons we used to be to grow up and mature into the persons God intended for us to be.

I look back on those years now, and I can view the moment with clearer lenses. Those two women passed the newspaper among the pews, and it irritated me no end. Perhaps they were really looking for a Word, an authentic Word, which I was unable to give. Jeremiah's question still rings true: "Is there any word from the Lord?" There is. It is a Word that will go through, whether by prophet, by preacher, or by the *Houston Post.*

If the *Houston Post* has the Word for the morning, so be it. Pass the newspaper, please!

Now upon the first day of the week, very early in the morning, they came unto the sepulchre, bringing the spices which they had prepared, and certain others with them. And they found the stone rolled away from the sepulchre. And they entered in, and found not the body of the Lord Jesus. And it came to pass, as they were much perplexed thereabout, behold, two men stood by them in shining garments: And as they were afraid, and bowed down their faces to the earth, they said unto them, Why seek ye the living among the dead? He is not here, but is risen!

LUKE 24:1–6

AN EASTER TO REMEMBER

Easter was more fun when I was a kid. Or maybe it's because I'm no longer a kid that I feel sort of shut out from the fun we used to have.

There was no more special day in the whole world than Easter—with the possible exception of Christmas, of course. But Easter was wonderful, especially when the weather would cooperate. With the sun beaming brightly from the moment we gathered for the traditional 6 A.M. service, followed by a healthy helping of Gladys Watkins' special-recipe scrambled eggs, Easter was wonderful.

Church would be packed at 9 o'clock because everybody had to be in place for the Sunday School Easter Program.

Do you remember when you had to learn your four-line poem for Easter Sunday and you stood in line, fidgety, anxious, excited, waiting for your turn to speak?

I greet you on this Easter morn
with poetry and prose.
My message now for you, my friend,
Jesus Christ arose!

And if you think that poem was bad, you should have heard the ones we really used.

But we loved it. We couldn't wait till it was over, of course, because the Sunday school would give all the children candy and

fruit and wonderful colored Easter eggs that we would promptly
take outside and throw at each other.

I hope I never forget what it was like to go to church on Easter
Sunday, with new shoes that squeaked and hurt when you walked,
and suits that Mama purchased too big so we could *"grow into
them"!* (There are some suits I don't think I *ever* grew into!)

The girls would wear their white dresses and have to sit still
because their mamas would kill them if they got those dresses
dirty. And all the women in the church would wear those humon-
gous hats with flowers and plastic fruit and veils, while the kids sat
in the balcony and snickered at how silly they all looked.

And was it hot! You never had "hot" like that! We didn't have
air-conditioning. The only "air-conditioning" was your fanning
back and forth with the paper fans from Whittaker's Funeral
Home. It was so hot in church you could see the steam coming
through the windows a half hour before church started. But you
wouldn't miss church on Easter Sunday. You loved it. There was
nothing like Easter Sunday down at old Mount Olivet on Main
Street.

But the Easter above all Easters came on a bright Sunday
morning in the early 1950s. It was a typical Easter—the church
jam-packed and hot. The people had come forty on a mule!
Everyone was there early for the devotions that started before the
main service began.

Deacon Douglas, Deacon Willis, and Deacon Watkins, sitting
in their seats on the left side of the pulpit, and the mothers of the
church seated on the right sure knew how to "stoke the fire" and
get the church ready for a Hallelujah service.

Midway in the devotions they called on the Reverend Jones to
pray. Now Reverend Jones was the closest thing my father had to
an assistant pastor. He had no formal training, and he was not for-
mally an employee of the church. You could count on him,
though, because he helped out where he could and was sincere
with everything he did. The kids thought Reverend Jones was sort
of an old fogy, but they liked him anyhow.

Reverend Jones stood to pray his Easter Sunday prayer. We
really didn't pay it much attention because he had prayed so often
that everybody in church had memorized his prayer.

Of course, nobody had a memorized prayer better than old Reverend Alec Alexander, who prayed the same prayer every Sunday the Lord sent him to us: "And, Lord, bless my mama-in-law where-some-never she may be!" Actually, the whole church stayed in an uproar because Reverend Alexander *never* knew the whereabouts of his mother-in-law!

But Reverend Jones was full stride in his prayer when all of a sudden . . . silence. He had stopped praying abruptly and, without saying so much as an "Amen" to close his prayer, nobody knew where Reverend Jones was. Reverend Jones had disappeared. We knew it was Easter Sunday morning but a disappearing preacher was a little much.

Finally, we spotted him. Reverend Jones was on his knees, actually on all-fours, under the center pulpit chair furiously groping and searching with both hands.

Those who had their eyes open during the prayer (you know I was not among that number!) told the real story: While Reverend Jones was praying with all his might, his dentures lost their grip and went sailing out across the pulpit,

over the white lilies on the flower stand

and under the center chair.

Reverend Jones had lost his teeth on Easter Sunday morning.

As news of the dearly departed teeth spread throughout the church—news travels swiftly under head-bowed bonnets—the congregation was in stitches, and it was all over for the rest of the day.

Forty years later, and I still remember Reverend Jones and his airborne teeth because I always thought there was probably a message in the events of that morning long ago. There is nothing wrong with the praying of our prayers. Even rehearsed, memorized prayers have their place, I suspect, when offered with sincerity and honesty.

In the pursuit of our religious devotions, however, we are in danger of spending so much time praying that our religion "loses its teeth."

To lose the teeth in our religion removes from us the power to speak and to proclaim the word of faith the world so desperately needs.

To lose the teeth in our religion places us in the position of mouthing the words without the power to be articulate in our prayers or our proclamation.

It runs the risk of our following form without producing faith.

It opens the possibility of doing the traditional, the accepted, but fails to bring us face to face with the resurrection possibility in our own lives.

We must never let habit take the bite out of our religion. We must never permit our Christianity to become commonplace or our spiritual senses to be dulled by the routine. What is there about your religion that challenges and confronts?

... that changes and converts?

... that disturbs and disrupts?

... that moves you beyond the ordinary,
the accepted, the expected?

We are a people of resurrection faith. Every Sunday is Easter Sunday. Every Sabbath moves us from funeral to festival. God be praised for a church that prays with the passion of Reverend Jones but in the process never loses the teeth, the substance, the power of its religion.

And Joshua had commanded the people, saying, Ye shall not shout, nor make any noise with your voice, neither shall any word proceed out of your mouth, until the day I bid you shout; then shall ye shout.

JOSHUA 6:10

WILSON MCCRAY'S SHOES

Deacon Henry Watkins made a declaration in his Sunday school class that would reverberate throughout the church for years to come. Declared Henry Watkins: "Konkaline Rules the World!" Now in case, dear reader, you have unfortunately led an underprivileged life and haven't a clue to what Konkaline was or is, let me enlighten you. In the early 1950s Konkaline was a chemical substance that was used to straighten the hair of black men. When a man had his hair "konked," it would come out shiny and wavy; actually the hair was quite straightened, glued, and plastered to the scalp, and in that time it was all the rage. Henry Watkins took the position that although the hair style was fashionable it was inappropriate for such church-going children as we, and therefore his commentary on hair styles stuck with him and the church for a long time.

Henry Watkins, however, was typical of some rather colorful characters who were our Sunday school teachers. My favorite of all time was Deacon James Walker, a kind man built like a giant, but with a gentle spirit. The Sunday school teacher I remember most, however, was Brother Wilson McCray.

Brother Wilson McCray was a fine and natty dresser. He was always appropriately dressed and, as I recall, always very punctual. Wilson McCray was a bachelor. We never knew much about him, where he worked, his family, or his home. Wilson McCray was sort of an anomaly. You never knew where he came from or where he was headed. You may be sure, however, that for all his limitations he was a faithful Sunday school teacher for me and for many other children as well.

Of particular note here is the fact that Wilson McCray loved to shout. He always sat on the aisle seat in about the fourth or fifth row from the front on the right. You could count on him. If you sat in the balcony in the right spot you could get an unobstructed view of the shouting Sunday school teacher.

You could just about time Wilson McCray with your watch. My father would be in full stride in his sermon, with maybe about fifteen minutes to go, and Wilson McCray could take it no longer. Up from his seat he would jump and begin his morning run. Wilson McCray would run around the church for all his life. Problem was, he always managed to leave his penny loafers neatly parked right by his newly deserted pew. There he goes...!

Wilson McCray would head due south to the rear of the church, picking up speed along the way, making a quick turn by the leaking radiator in the corner,

down the side aisle to make a screeching left by the Deaconess Board across the front of the church,

snaking his way at breakneck speed through the Deacons' area, his necktie fanning out across his forehead

(the choir on its feet, the front row of the balcony leaning precariously so as not to miss one "bob" or one "weave," urging the peripatetic Mr. McCray on his journey),

down the other aisle, turning startled ushers in his wake,

back across the rear of the sanctuary,

sometimes making a detour out into the vestibule,

and then back down the center aisle where he would properly and appropriately take his Holy-Ghost-filled, sanctified seat with nary a drop of sweat on his brow to show for it.

While I share this with you in humorous reverie, let me assure you that what was at work here was serious. We never knew the strain or the struggle that Wilson McCray experienced during his week. He could have been a porter, a street sweep, or a holder of some other menial task. Whatever his lot, by the time he arrived in church on Sunday he had had enough and was determined, no matter what, to let it out.

It is also worthy of note that we never knew Wilson McCray to be depressed; you never saw him with his head hung down; you never heard of a visit to the local state mental hospital. (We called it "the Hilltop" in Columbus!) Whatever therapy he needed in order to endure his lot in life, he received it on Sunday morning, on the fourth or fifth row from the front on the right on the center aisle. When Wilson McCray left his shoes, he left his burdens, his trials, his faults, his failures, his tears, and his sorrows. And I imagine when Wilson McCray shouted and left his shoes in place I imagine God smiled. In fact, in my imagination, I imagine God shouted with him.

Now then, from my perspective, I believe that religion was never intended to be lifeless and morose. While you may not understand or appreciate the shouting mentality, I, for one, do not believe that religion was intended to be cold, dry, lifeless, lethargic, monotonous, inert, unmoving, comatose, unbending, unyielding, sorrow stained, tear filled, or dead.

I am convinced that there is something wrong whenever those who claim to be the children of God gather in the same place at the same time every Lord's Day morning for the purpose of singing sad songs to people who look sad and listening to sermons that sound sad, preached by preachers who are sad, and then claim they went to church and had a good time.

I am convinced that there is something fundamentally wrong when those who claim to be among the called and the converted think that religion is designed to make them look as if they just lost their best friend or dress like they're on their way to their own funeral, or to make them sit in one place, never smile, never get happy, keep their mouths shut, and then go home in one hour just as messed up when they go out as they were when they came in.

I am convinced, quite to the contrary, that authentic religion, the Gospel, the good news of Jesus Christ is designed to fill you; it is designed to saturate you; it is designed to cleanse you; it is designed to take the broken pieces of your life and put you back together again; and it is designed to open you up, set you free, liberate you, give you hope and help for the living of one more day and, as a consequence of your religious rooting and grounding, every once in a while if your religion is real, even with your high-tone, high-class, bourgeois, sophisticated self, you ought to have something to shout about. And Wilson McCray agreed.

By the way, perhaps what really happened was that Wilson McCray read his Bible:

"And he said, Draw not nigh hither: put off thy shoes from off thy feet, for the place whereon thou standest is holy ground" (Exodus 3:5).

God grant that we, like Wilson McCray, may become so free, so liberated, so unencumbered with the expected and the accepted, that as Hebrews 12:1 puts it, we will be able, if only in our imagination, to "lay aside every weight, and the sin which doth so easily beset us, and let us run ... !"

THE PREACHER ON THE PORCH

The year was 1970, and A. D. King was dead. The year was 1970, and the nation was still reeling from the deaths of Martin King; Bobby Kennedy; and Mama King, shot while playing the Lord's Prayer on the Ebenezer Church organ. And now A. D., Martin's brother, was dead.

I had a debt to pay. I needed to go to A. D. King's funeral because he was one of the first to give me an opportunity to preach when, though I didn't know it at the time, I hardly knew what preaching was. Two days after my marriage to my beautiful bride, the former Elizabeth Harrison of Selma, Alabama, I preached in the West Hunter Street Baptist Church, pastored then by A. D. King. Liz and I had lots of love and little money, but A. D. helped us on the way.

My plane landed at Hartsfield International Airport in Atlanta well before the time of the service. I took a taxi to the church and then I began just wandering the streets, with no particular destination in mind. It was early morning, and Auburn Avenue was beginning to stir. The hot summer sun had already turned the sidewalks into steaming slabs underfoot. The sights, the sounds, the smells of the South were all around.

It was here that I had my first opportunity to see the famous Wheat Street Baptist Church and its famous towers of high-rise accommodations for senior citizens. These towers were then the model of Black church activity and would prevail as the paradigm for years to come.

As I walked around the Wheat Street Church I noticed a little house nearby. The house had no remarkable features; it was typical of homes of the community. Then I noticed, there on the porch, a gray-haired, distinguished-looking gentleman. No one had to tell me who it was; I wondered if I dared approach him to speak. Quite tentatively I stood at the gate in the front yard. We spoke and passed pleasantries of the morning.

"Dr. Borders, I am H. Beecher Hicks Jr., Pastor of the Mount Ararat Baptist Church in Pittsburgh, Pennsylvania."

"And how are you, sir?"

"Fine, sir. Is it possible that I might speak with you for a moment?"

"Come right on up. Have a seat here on the porch, and we'll talk."

There I was. Smack dab in the middle of a moment far beyond my wildest imaginations. I was actually speaking with William Holmes Borders, a pulpit giant, a published author, the "Prophet of Wheat Street" himself, a living legend.

For the next few moments William Holmes Borders had become more than a preacher on the porch, he had become a confidant, a mentor, a friend. In typical southern fashion he asked me who my "people" were, what I was doing in Atlanta, and what I was doing in Pittsburgh, and on and on.

William Holmes Borders took the time to share something of himself with me. He did not know me, and he had no particular interest in me; I was the pastor of a church he did not know. Yet I found in him a willingness to be real and to share the insights of a ministry that had lasted twice as long as I was old. I will never forget his brief but meaningful investment in me.

Since that morning I've been on the front porch of a lot of preachers. Every preacher needs to find another preacher on the porch.

H. Beecher Hicks Sr., my father in the faith and in the flesh, had a broad front porch. He modeled for me what it meant to be a pastor, more pastor than I will ever be. I learned more by his example than I could ever learn by academic pursuit.

James Alvin Sanders, eminent Old Testament scholar, never remembered my name in seminary. And he would never know that to this day I refer to his lecture notes, his writings, for insight into the Scriptures.

Gene E. Bartlett and J. C. Wynn opened to me the wonder of the written Word. I have never forgotten their patience or the instruction of their example.

William Augustus Jones, friend and brother, perhaps more than any other opened my eyes to the power of the preaching craft. I remember that night in the Baptist Temple Church in Pittsburgh, Pennsylvania, when this behemoth of a preacher preached with such awesome power on the subject "Revolutionary Preaching." I remember his opening line: "Amos is my favorite prophet." William Jones revealed for me the art of preaching with elegance and grace, the word crafted with alliterative skill, the Spirit anointment, the blending of scholarship with soul and, as he would say it, of "faith with feeling." All of these qualities would from that day to this indelibly mark my own feeble preaching.

There are so many other porches on which I have spent the mornings of my spiritual search, longing and searching for that mystery of the faith that enriches and empowers those who have been touched by coals from the altar. All of us, whether preachers or teachers or whatever we may be, need someone on whose porch we can sit in order to gain perspective, in order to measure ourselves with something that is beyond ourselves.

All of this is important, of course, because although my ministry began with a sure and certain "call," there is no doubt in my mind that God sent me from porch to porch in order that he might fulfill the essence of my own imagination and make me that which he first imagined me to be. God charted my course through unknown waters and then provided the wisdom of seasoned sailors whose guidance would be a part of my anchoring system in years to come. And it takes some imagination still to imagine me a preacher.

I don't know when I first imagined myself a preacher. I only know that from the moment of my call, my experience with the Eternal, there was never any question, no crisis of identity around the claim that had been placed on my life. I never imagined the church, I never imagined the city, I never imagined the trappings of this peculiar office. I only imagined that in some strange way God could use me to do a work for him.

Ah, yes, I also sat on the porch of the late A. Edward Davis, then pastor of the Calvary Church of Chicago, Illinois. I remember speaking with him one afternoon following a Religious Emphasis Week sermon on the AM&N campus. My question for him was a simple one. With all my faults, all my failures, how could God possibly use me? How could God possibly find a way to justify calling me as a preacher?

While I sat on A. Edward Davis's porch he reminded me that God's work is larger than I am. God has a way, he assured me, of using us in spite of us. Even more, he went on to say, everyone God called was not qualified for the job.

Noah was a drunk.

Abraham was a liar.

Moses was a murderer.

David was a philanderer.

Jeremiah was a crybaby.

Samson was a ladies' man.

Matthew was an extortioner.

Thomas was a doubter.

Peter was a man who denied his Lord.

Every preacher God called never quite deserved the title. But God called undeserving preachers and used them, in spite of what they were. God looked beyond what they were to what they could become.

There is now within me a sense of dread and joy as I enter this second half-century of my life. I have already experienced both of those emotions as I have begun to see preachers, male and female, come to sit on the porch of my experience. What shall I tell them—these new proclaimers, prophets, and prophetesses of the Word? I am confident that I have not lived up to the models set before me, nor have I appropriately integrated the lessons of their ministries into my own. Yet across these years I have tried to share with others my triumph and my tears. I imagine that God will receive and honor them both. Now that I sit on this porch of my own reflection I am pleased to remember that "imperfection is the wound that lets God in!"[3]

I am confident that I have not become that which God imagined me to be. As a preacher, as a person, I am yet under construction, a work in progress. Still, it is in these hours of my alone-ness that I find myself under God's gaze, under his guiding hand. I will become what he intends for me to become. Until then I will sit on the porch of God, converse with God's Son, be confirmed by God's Spirit, share my fears, my frustrations, my failures. There, on God's porch, I am confident I will hear God say:

"Be still and know that I am God."

God is our refuge and strength, a very present help in trouble. There-fore will not we fear, though the earth be removed, and though the mountains be carried into the midst of the sea; Though the waters therof roar and be troubled, though the mountains shake with the swelling thereof.

PSALM 46:1–3

O God, our help in ages past,
  Our hope for years to come,
  Our shelter from the stormy blast,
  And our eternal home.

ISAAC WATTS

MY SOUL'S BEEN ANCHORED

*I*f the truth be known, there has never been a time when preaching was not on the agenda of my life. Born the grandson and the son of preachers, it is as though preaching is a part of my genes, my spiritual DNA; it is a fact of my life that cannot be escaped.

Earlier on I said that preaching was not my personal preference. Indeed, for the first sixteen years of my life I absolutely abhorred the notion. As I recall considering the vocational options for my life, I never imagined that I would ever mount the stairs of any pulpit or see my name displayed in the garish lights of a church marquee.

During the years of my childhood I saw enough preachers to last a lifetime. I did not much appreciate it then, but now I remember fondly those days when preachers from all over the world would come to stay in our home, to eat at our table, and to share their wonderful stories. The bitter truth is that I was quite grown before I knew that a chicken had any part other than the one that was the last to go over the fence.

As I look on it, these preachers taught me a lot. A preacher from Texas took time to teach me how to blow my nose properly. A preacher from Colorado, the Reverend Dr. Wendell T. Liggins as I recall, took time to teach me how to make a shoeshine box from wood scraps in the basement and then how to shine my shoes. A preacher from Pittsburgh initiated me into the "I will arise and go to my Father" fraternity! I remember long evenings in the presence of Sandy Ray, Gardner Taylor, J. A. Bacoats, Martin Luther King Jr., and so many, many more. I really had nothing to do with becoming a preacher. My life was marked, the path set, my destiny predetermined by the hand of the Divine.

> *Then the word of the LORD came unto me, saying, Before I formed thee in the belly, I knew thee; and before thou camest forth out of the womb I sanctified thee, and I ordained thee a prophet unto the nations. . . .*
>
> *Be not afraid of their faces: for I am with thee to deliver thee, saith the LORD. Then the LORD put forth his hand, and touched my mouth. And the LORD said unto me, Behold, I have put my words in thy mouth.*

JEREMIAH 1:4–5, 8–9

The influences on my spiritual life were far more personal and far more frequent than those of the preachers who occasionally entered into my life. Most of those who shaped and molded me were persons most of whom had never been to school, some of whom could not read or write their names, but all of whom flooded my life with a love that literally would not let me go.

My father was called to the pastorate of the Mount Olivet Church in Columbus, Ohio, in 1946. At the time I was only three years old, but I remember as though it were yesterday the old, semi-Victorian structure with fascinating stained-glass windows complete with a blue-eyed Jesus in nearly every frame knocking on a door or shepherding the sheep. Even then the church was shaking from age, and the crowds who filled her every week simply added to the strain. The church had only one janitor, old Grady Moore, who doubled as "Chief Chef and Head Bottle Washer" every Sunday after church.

We lived in a parsonage provided by the church. We were perhaps one of only a few families who lived in a home where they were not paying rent, a rarity in those days to live without a party wall or a party telephone line. Truth of the matter is, the members of the church took ownership of the parsonage quite seriously. Bear in mind that church services lasted all day—Sunday school at 9, morning worship at 10:45, afternoon worship with a visiting church at 3:30, B.Y.P.U. (Baptist Young People's Union) at 6 o'clock, followed by evening worship at 7:30. Many a Sunday evening I was carried home sound asleep on my daddy's shoulders.

In between the morning worship, which usually ended around 1 o'clock, and the afternoon worship, which began at 3:30, many members of the congregation had little to do and nowhere to go. The church did not have a "lounge," but they did have a parsonage only about two blocks away. Much to my mother's regret, our living room became the Sunday afternoon place to be. The women of the church would sort of "drop by" the parsonage on Sunday afternoon, take off their hats and their shoes, and sit down for a spell.

"Now, don't you mind us, Dear. You just go right on with what you're doing! Don't you pay us no mind at all."

Of course, I thought it was a perfect arrangement. The little old ladies from the church, many of whom were members of the Pastor's Aide led by the venerable Ethel Clark, who could make the meanest Floating Island custard you will ever taste in life, composed an eager audience, ripe for entertainment that I absolutely could not resist.

It wouldn't be long before someone would say,

"Little Henry, come here."

"Yes, ma'am."

"Tell us what your Daddy preached today!"

That's all I needed. Quicker than a flash I would go into my one-man review of everything I had heard in the morning service. I would preach, just as I remembered it, everything I heard my daddy say, complete with sound effects, amens, and appropriate gesticulations. They loved it. I loved it. What could be better on a Sunday afternoon?

Soon the ladies got an idea. Since I was preaching, I needed to have my own robe and my own pulpit. So, at about age four, I was given my very own hand-made robe and placed precariously for preaching atop my mother's living room Duncan Phyfe coffee table. I was the Sunday afternoon boy preacher they came from everywhere to see and, as they say, the rest is history.

Gardner Taylor of the Concord Church in Brooklyn, New York, suggested in his *Lyman Beecher Lectures* that preaching "is a

clumsy tool" placed in the hands of those who are ill-equipped to use it. Yet it is by this thing called preaching that one person is used of God to call men and women into a new covenantal relationship with the Eternal. It is by this thing called preaching that the vision for a new heaven and a new earth comes more clearly into focus and the center of mission is found and forged. It is by this thing called preaching that a divine-human partnership is formed, such that our shoes must be removed, our faces hid. It is by this thing called preaching that both preacher and people are molded and disciplined to become a new community, a *koinonia* marked by the *charis,* the love, the grace of God.

All great preaching lives by three realities: imagination, integrity, and blood. I do not know how many Sunday morning prayers I have heard that called upon God to "turpentine" the preacher's imagination. James Weldon Johnson in his classic "Listen, Lord—A Prayer" writes of old Negro prayers:

> *And now, O Lord, this man of God,*
> *Who breaks the bread of Life this morning—*
> *Shadow him in the hollow of thy hand,*
> *And keep him out of the gunshot of the devil.*
> *Take him, Lord—this morning—*
> *Wash him with hyssop inside and out,*
> *Hang him up and drain him dry of sin.*
> *Pin his ear to the wisdom-post,*
> *And make his words sledgehammers of truth—*
> *Beating on the iron heart of sin.*
> *Lord God, this morning—*
> *Put his eye to the telescope of eternity,*
> *And let him look upon the paper walls of time.*
> *Lord, turpentine his imagination,*
> *Put perpetual motion in his arms,*
> *Fill him with the dynamite of thy power,*
> *Anoint him all over with the oil of thy salvation,*
> *And set his tongue on fire.*

It is the *imagination,* we often call it "sanctified imagination," that God uses to take what appears to be ordinary,
    the ordinary circumstances of life,

the ordinary predicaments of life,
    the ordinary preaching of life,
and so set it in the minds of others that it takes on a new reality, a new power to change and to renew. It is the "turpentine" of the spirit that so sets in motion, invigorates, enlivens, and cleanses the soul of the preacher that that soul can be used over and over again to be the vessel through which God's Word may be poured anew.

This thing called preaching finds its power in its integrity. I break no new ground here to suggest that authentic preaching does not come from the mouth, it comes from the feet. With my mouth I might say almost anything, but with my feet I verify my words by the actions of my life. It is, indeed, a brand new walk. Authentic preaching is not a thing to be said, it is a life to be lived. While we preach the faith, the faith must live in us.

While we preach of grace, that grace must be infused into our lives and into our relationships with others.

While we must preach of forgiveness, there is yet an imperative to acknowledge our own need for forgiveness and to share it liberally with others.

William Augustus Jones has suggested more than once that there can be no serious preaching unless it has "blood on it." He speaks eloquently and well to the reality that those who preach cannot do so without pain, without suffering. He speaks to the essence of Henry Nouwen's *Wounded Healer,*[4] strangely setting forth the reality that those who would heal others must first be healed. There is no need for healing, however, where there has been no hurt, where there has been no wound. It is, then, out of my sense of "woundedness" that I come to the pulpit to have reflected in my life and in my preaching the messianic characteristic—"a man of sorrows, acquainted with grief." Our preaching, to be real, must bleed the blood that marked the doorposts of slave huts in Egypt, the blood that flowed from Calvary's tree, the blood of slave ships and the whip-lashed backs of my ancestors. It is with this blood that I gain a seminal connection between my heritage, my history, and my hope.

Ah, but there is a price to be paid for such preaching. It is a price that is extracted on the anvil of human hurt. It is a price that is paid through misunderstood motives, false accusation, the treachery of friends, illusive dreams, dreams deferred, moments of depression, days of doubt, spiritual anxiety, and sometimes even the loss of faith.

And yet, we do not stand alone. Matthew closes his Gospel with the promise of the presence of Jesus, a promise for disciples then and now:

All power is given unto me in heaven and in earth.

Go ye therefore, and teach all nations, baptizing them in the name of the Father, and of the Son, and of the Holy Ghost: Teaching them to observe all things whatsoever I have commanded you: and, lo, I am with you alway, even unto the end of the world. Amen.

MATTHEW 28:18–20

It was in a late-night telephone conversation with my friend and brother, the Reverend Thomas L. Rogers of the Triumphant Church in Hyattsville, Maryland, that he pointed out a preaching value in this Scripture that I had never seen. He pointed out that the phrase "I am with you ..." comes from the Greek *ego meth' hymon eimi,* which literally translated is, "I with you I am," or, more freely, "I, myself, am with you." It is almost as though Jesus paused to emphasize His statement when He said, "I, myself," or, to put it another way, *"It's me, it's me!"*

When, in the moment of the preacher's deepest distress, when his preaching is poor and there appears to be no response in the pew and when, at the same time, there is a power to preach that comes from an unknown source, there is yet to be heard that whispering voice, *"It's me, it's me!"* When forces of opposition appear to be ever present, when you are misunderstood, when you appear to have only broken and clumsy tools and yet at the same time there is born within you a courage to persevere and a strength to endure, there is yet that haunting refrain, *"It's me, it's me!"*

Some years ago I revealed times of pain in my ministry, pain that I could only describe by the phrase "preaching through a storm." It is true that across more than three decades of preaching I have known the ebb and flow of ministry, the rising and the falling of life's storms. The storm motif, so strong and illustrative of our sojourn together, is now, I think, woven into the spiritual

fabric of the congregation I presently serve. And yet the storms
we have faced and will face are not seen as depressive factors of
life; they have become the source of an increase of our faith, our
joy, and our hope.

> *Though the storms keep on raging in my life*
> *and sometimes it's hard to tell the night from day,*
> *Still that hope that lies within is reassured*
> *as I keep my eye upon that distant shore—*
> *I know He'll lead me safely to*
> *that blessed place He has prepared.*
> *And if the storms won't cease,*
> *And if the winds keep on blowing in my life,*
> *My soul has been anchored in the Lord!*[5]

PART *Four*

IMAGINE DEATH, IMAGINE LIFE

Strange, isn't it, that death is required so that life can be lived? Death shows us the things we thought we lost but never had. Life shows us that death is really an imposter, our failures are not fatal, and new life is only a moment away. Death shows us that when tomorrow comes, resurrection is real. If we will only permit some ideas, some failures, some habits to die, how soon will we be engulfed in the abundant life God has prepared. Those who grasp the life-giving, life-sustaining essence of the teachings of Jesus Christ have found for themselves an anchor that holds during even the most severest storm. Imagine death? No, imagine life!

*I will lift up mine eyes unto the hills, from whence cometh my help.
My help cometh from the LORD, which made heaven and earth. He will
not suffer thy foot to be moved: he that keepeth thee will not slumber.
Behold, he that keepeth Israel shall neither slumber nor sleep.*

*The LORD is thy keeper: the LORD is thy shade upon thy right hand.
The sun shall not smite thee by day, nor the moon by night. The LORD
shall preserve thee from all evil: he shall rpeserve thy soul. The LORD
shall preserve thy going out and thy coming in from this time forth, and
even for evermore.*

PSALM 121

THE DEATH OF IMAGINATION

*I've really got to use my imagination
to think of good reasons to keep on hanging on!*

GLADYS KNIGHT

The gothic cathedral imposed itself against the frigid Boston
skyline. Its steeple shining, the gleaming cross aloft, I stepped from
my taxi and quickly made my way across the esplanade in full
anticipation of worship. Subtly, almost imperceptibly, my attention was drawn to the statue in honor of Martin Luther King, Jr. No
doubt about it, I had come to the right place.

My goal was simple: to be able to worship in the context of
community and to be stimulated both intellectually and spiritually.

I was seeking something different from my typical Sunday
fare.

Something different, but enriching ... powerful and empowering, but *not* so different that I would not be brought face to face
with the Christ of God and the God within.

I came genuinely hungering and thirsting, needing a Word
from the Lord; I wanted to be drawn again to Calvary.

I would sit among the students and try to sense the emotions
that might be uncovered. I would sit among them, as one of them,
and argue mentally with the preacher's position and quickly take
a position of my own. There among the pews, just one pew away

from the last, instead of publicly praying for others, I would be present so that someone else could pray for me.

And sing. I wanted to sing. I wanted to stand and sing, full-throated, the great hymns of the faith. I did not want to choose the hymns. I did not want to lead the hymns. I wanted to be ministered to through the hymns. I wanted to hear the Gregorian chants and listen to the soaring anthem of an excellent collegiate choir.

Most of all, I wanted to learn. I wanted to sit at the feet of a religious scholar-preacher whose daily assignment it is to

communicate the Gospel to a contemporary culture out of control;

whose daily challenge it is to

speak to the ideas and ideologies of a generation of young people who seem to have so little regard for that which has gone before;

whose daily charge it is to

address in creative and imaginative manner the conflicts that mark our culture

and mark our time.

I was not prepared for what I saw . . . for what I sensed.

A magnificent cathedral nearly empty.

Young people, children by the measure of my years, worshipers with the blank stares of boredom and disinterest,

empty spirits;

lifeless singing, notes that came from the printed score and not from impassioned hearts;

prayers reflective of the identity crisis of God . . . in one prayer God being referred to as grandfather, grandmother, father, mother, sister, brother.

Still more . . . what pained me more . . . was the lifeless, powerless, imaginationless preaching. I watched and listened to the preacher, but as I glanced about me it was obvious that hardly a soul paid any attention to what the preacher had to say. In the place where now, more than ever, the Gospel must be proclaimed with purity and with power what is found is an

anemic . . . impotent . . . infertile pulpit

in the presence of an

inert . . . feeble . . . unredemptive

society of spiritual sameness that we dare call the church of Jesus Christ.

In the place where now, more than ever, men and women come questioning with Jeremiah, "Is there any word from the LORD?" the response is neither yes nor no—it is the insulting sound of silence. We have not heard, therefore we cannot speak.

When did imagination die?

What happened to the spiritual ear, able to hear and translate the whisperings of the Word?

What happened to the spiritual eye, able to see far beyond the plane of mortal men?

What happened to the cry of prophets who spoke the Word of God so graphically that kingdoms rose and fell?

What happened to what James Weldon Johnson called that "turpentined imagination" that could sense and see and hear what God was saying and doing and—in the translation to the tongue and ears of mortal men—so excite those who heard the Word that they would literally rise to their feet and march out to "turn the world upside down"?

Is it any wonder that a pall of hopelessness has overtaken our generation?

Is it any wonder that our children are more suicidal now than at any other time in the history of humankind?

Is it any wonder that our times are more violent than any other period of history ?

Is it not because we have failed to preach the Gospel of peace ... and hope ... and affirmation ... and victory?

I see on every corner of this city, churches of every denomination and every description. And I notice, almost without exception, wrought-iron gates that have been erected around them. I wonder if the gates are there to keep God in or to keep God out. Maybe the gates have nothing to do with God. Maybe the gates have only to do with the lack of our imagination to bring the world in and to show it that God cares or to let the church out to demonstrate that God lives.

One ought not to be critical of those who minister in ways that fulfill their sense of call and spiritual destiny. The Gospel is surely

preached by more means and methods than one. Still, in these
desperate times, in these critical times, we cannot be content with
a ministry of the common or the commonplace; we cannot be content with those who preach with no urgency, no zeal, no fire. Hear
my ancestors sing in slave fields:

> *Time is winding up,*
> *'Struction's in the land;*
> *God's gonna move His hand,*
> *Time is winding up!*

So I went to the chapel, perhaps idealistically so, seeking to be
inspired and fulfilled. I should have known that typically one does
not go to the citadels of higher learning to be spiritually fed. I
knew, cerebrally at least, that the college chapel is not necessarily
the habitat of the Holy. As a consequence, I left empty and
depressed and sad. I walked across the empty esplanade trying
desperately to hail down a moving cab. I could hardly see as I was
walking, for as I walked, I cried.

What a tragedy it may be to discover that the obituary of the
twentieth-century church may record that the culture died while
the church did nothing creative, nothing redemptive, nothing
imaginative to save the culture or to save the church. Perhaps the
obituary of the church will be that it floated off in some ecclesiastical bathtub, without oar, without rudder, without anchor.

And Peter went out, and wept bitterly.

LUKE 22:62

THE DEATH OF FAILURE

In every life there is always some mark of failure. No matter how impressive our résumés, no matter how glowing our reviews, no matter how convinced we are that we have the superior ability to be "all things to all people," all of us who are by birth mere mortals have experienced that common denominator of life we call failure. Such is surely the case in your life, such is surely the case in my own.

As I pen these words on failure there is an emotion of both pain and relief that sweeps over me. These are words I have never before written, a story I have not shared with my closest friends. With these words I literally release the skeleton from my closet.

I was only fourteen years old when I entered my first oratorical contest. The Ohio Council of Churches sponsored what was then known as the Prince of Peace Contest; it was open to high school students who had memorized orations on the subject of peace. On my first try, I won the prize and was awarded a full four-year scholarship to any of eight Ohio colleges. The choice was mine to make.

The September following my graduation ahead of schedule from Columbus East High School I entered Wittenberg College in Springfield, Ohio. A Lutheran school, Wittenberg was close enough to home and yet far enough away for me to feel a sense of freedom and independence. I entered my freshman year full of confidence and was not at all deterred by the fact that of sixteen hundred students only seven were black. Wittenberg was known as the "Harvard of the Midwest." I had been accepted, and I was certain to do well.

While going to college was expected of me and I had received a scholarship, it was still a great honor. I was required to work my

way to get there, to buy my clothes, and to buy my books; my parents wanted to be sure that I was invested in this process. So I sold newspapers. On my bicycle I delivered prescriptions for Tyler Drug Store at twenty cents a delivery. I even drove the ambulance and the hearse for Crosby's Funeral Home, picking up the dead and delivering them to the embalming table in the back room. Going off to college meant something to me then, perhaps far more than it means to children today.

Unfortunately, I did not do well my first year. My academic efforts never seemed to match the expectations of my professors, no matter how diligently I tried, no matter how diligently I studied. I would learn in later years that my father was informed by the college dean that Wittenberg was really not designed for youngsters of my "kind" and that I would probably do well elsewhere.

Undeterred, I continued to struggle, meeting with modest success. In the summer following my freshman year my average *was* average as I recall. While I really was depressed about the record of my performance, my singing skill had been discovered, and Professor Miller, director of the famous Wittenberg Choir, with whom I traveled to Europe in the summer of 1961, decided that I was worth an investment and offered me a scholarship to continue my studies there.

However, I was not happy. My parents expected more of me. I expected more of myself. Then the thought of transferring to another college came to mind, and I began the process of making application to other colleges. In point of fact, however, I really wanted to go to only one other college–Morehouse College in Atlanta, Georgia.

My Uncle Jake and Aunt Missy had made a trip to Columbus from Baton Rouge in the summer of '61 and we were all seated at the dining room table when the postman arrived. A letter from Morehouse College signed by the registrar, one Cookie Hamilton, offered the following information:

Dear Mr. Hicks:

> We regret to inform you upon review of your record that we will not be able to admit you to the Morehouse College.

Devastated, I stood on the front porch and cried. My mother was a graduate of Spelman. My Uncle Jake and Uncle Harold were both graduates of Morehouse. My family was a family of college graduates, of educators, and I was denied admission to Morehouse. Humiliation, added to a sense of failure, was more than I could take.

Uncle Bud, my father's brother, Dr. Charles A. Hicks, was a graduate of the AM&N College in Pine Bluff, Arkansas, and had a position in secondary education with the state. I didn't know much about the school except that Uncle Bud graduated from there. My brother Billy and I traveled to Arkansas in the summer months by train to be with Uncle Bud, always delighted to hear the conductor cry out the names of the cities, always placing the accent on the wrong syllable: "Terra Hoe Tay!" (Terre Haute).

So Uncle Bud made the appropriate calls, and I was on my way for my first extended stay in the rural south. I would excel here, recovering the damage done by my freshman-year grades. I took a correspondence course with Henderson State College in order to erase that F in World History, miraculously graduating cum laude. Achieving that success, giving leadership to civil rights demonstrations, rising among my peers to become president of the student body, I had found the illusion of success, but the pain of that first failure, quite honestly, haunted me day and night.

Once the prospect of seminary loomed into my view, I knew I would have to go north, to a predominantly white institution to prove, if only to myself, that I could make it in an academic world that I felt had mistreated and rejected me. As time and chance would have it, I received two degrees from Colgate Rochester Divinity School, completed additional work at the University of Rochester, and received a fellowship from Harvard Divinity School. I could finally assure myself that I do have a mind, I can compete, I do have value and worth, and I do have something to contribute. I never knew that God had imagined all of this for me.

Our sons had their own decisions to make. Henry was offered a scholarship to a military academy but turned it down. Ivan sent an application to only one college. Both our sons, however, were determined to go to Morehouse. I never told them how secretly proud I was of their decisions, and even though they had no scholarship support, their mother and I worked for the six years of their matriculation to insure that without scholarships or grants, when they graduated they would have no student loans to pay, no debts to resolve. We paid with our sweat and our love for their college education—every last dime!

Our sons were doing well. Henry had received a job with the Monsanto Company in St. Louis, and Ivan had become the president of the senior class. It was then that I received my second letter from Morehouse College:

> Dear Dr. Hicks:
>
> It is my privilege to invite you to be the guest speaker for the Baccalaureate service for the Class of 1991 in the Martin Luther King Memorial Chapel on the campus of the college.
>
> Sincerely,
> Dr. Lawrence Carter, Dean of the Chapel

Without hesitation, I accepted the invitation.

I confess, my emotions were clear. I had been rejected once but now—in this strange twisting of human events that could only come from the imagination of God—now I would address those who would not accept me as a student so many, many years ago. I came bearing gifts: a check for five thousand dollars to place a communion table in the chapel in memory of my sainted mother and a determination to preach with every fiber of my being until the very walls of that chapel shook. I came to that chapel with a determination to speak to those graduates on the subject "The Phenomenon of Flight," to encourage them to soar beyond the limitations of their environment, above the restrictions of any who would dare to tell them what they could not do or could not become. It was indeed a bittersweet moment of vindication and joy. I shall never forget the day. I shall never forget the hour.

Now I must face the real question: What is failure? Is failure the inability to measure up to the standards that others have set for us, or the inability to measure up to the standards we have set for ourselves? Is failure a consequence of doing something wrong, or is it to come face to face with the acknowledgment that we are not as close to perfection as we had imagined ourselves to be? Is failure really our fear that we will be unable to stand above our peers, to cross over into the unknown, and to come just short of our original intention? Perhaps.

Benjamin Mays, president of Morehouse College, suggested to his students that not failure, but low aim is sin. I suspect, however, that real failure is the inability to let failure die. The real failure is the inability to learn the lessons of the past and then press the "fast forward" button of the mind and move on with one's life. The real failure is to be so caught up in the reverie of the past that one fails to see or appreciate what God has imagined for our future. What God has given us is a mixture of trial and error, of pain and pleasure, of joy and sorrow. Still, God imagines a new you, a new me, a new world. That new world is born the day failure dies.

Imagine death? No, imagine life.

"For I know the plans I have for you," declares the LORD, "plans to prosper you and not to harm you, plans to give you hope and a future. Then you will call upon me and come and pray to me, and I will listen to you. You will seek me and find me when you seek me with all your heart."

JEREMIAH 29:11–13 NIV

As an eagle stirreth up her nest, fluttereth over her young, spreadeth abroad her wings, taketh them, beareth them on her wings:
So the LORD alone did lead him, and there was no strange god with him.

DEUTERONOMY 32:11–12

For most gulls, it is not flying that matters but eating. For this gull, though, it was not eating that mattered but flight.

RICHARD BACH, JONATHAN LIVINGSTON SEAGULL[1]

THE PHENOMENON OF FLIGHT

*I*magine for a moment that we are all students—as indeed we are. Even if we are not enrolled at Morehouse College or some other institution of higher learning, we are full-time students in the University of Life, the School of Hard Knocks. The course is flying—learning how to fly, how to stay aloft. And the Divine Professor is about to give an exam on the phenomenon of flight.[2]

The legacy of the Old Testament is that it seeks to define and to illumine the relationship of the creature to the Creator. Throughout the history of humankind, from the splendor on the morning of creation, in spite of the appearance of sin under the shade trees of Eden's garden, because of the burden of bondage of slavery in Egypt, motivated by the miraculous parting of the sea, lifted by the giving of the law and blessed by the burning of that bush on Mount Sinai, and even to that moment when Israel crossed over into the Promised Land, the *Creator* is always in the process of defining His relationship with that which He has *created.*

The Old Testament is, at its core, a divine record designed to make clear who God is, what God does, and how God acts in human history. The pages of this old book, worn by the waste of years, tell of a God who is sensitive to hurt, who understands man's predicament of pain—a God who is filled with compassion, whose love is without limit, and whose grace is guaranteed. It is the story not of how *man* chose God, but of how *God* chose man.

Moses wrote the words found in Deuteronomy 32:9–12:

For the LORD's portion is his people; Jacob is the lot of his inheritance. He found him in a desert land, and in the waste howling wilderness; he led him about, he instructed him, he kept him as the apple of his eye. As an eagle stirreth up her nest, fluttereth over her young, spreadeth abroad her wings, taketh them, beareth them on her wings: So the LORD alone did lead him, and there was no strange god with him.

These words do not come in the morning of Moses' life. They do not come from those tender years of his adolescent maturation in Pharaoh's palace. They do not come from those lonely years of sojourn in Midian with the flocks of Jethro around Mount Horeb. They do not come from those anxious years of sober reflection and remembrance of that day when he killed an Egyptian taskmaster with his own hands. These are the tempered and thoughtful words of an old man—an old man who is able to look back upon a relationship with God. He knew what God had done for him. When Moses spoke of Israel and God, he was at the same time talking about Moses and God....

Moses knew, by virtue of his own healthy sense of realism, that the relationship of God and Israel was ruptured. Israel had forsaken and forgotten God. The nation had become corrupt. The social order suffered from collective spiritual amnesia and could not remember that God and Israel had signed a cosmic contract: "I will be your God and you shall be My people."...

This is the song that Moses sang. God is like an eagle, and He finds us, He owns us, He protects us, He shelters us, He provides for us, He instructs us, He looks out for us, He loves us, and, Moses said, "He kept him as the apple of his eye"—in spite of us!

Moses does not speak of this relationship between Israel and God by obvious and pedestrian means. There is something deeper here, a profundity and depth that moves beyond a surface analysis of Israel's situation. A more definitive word is needed to describe the relationship of God with humanity; as a consequence, Moses becomes metaphorical. He says that God is to Israel what an eagle is to her young:

As an eagle stirreth up her nest,
fluttereth over her young,

spreadeth abroad her wings, taketh them,
beareth them on her wings:
So the LORD alone did lead him,
and there was no strange god with him.

I am drawn to this image if for no other reason than the fact that it would appear that we have entered an era when *the eagle is an endangered species.* The eagle, for Moses and for us, is both a metaphor and a paradigm of who we are, who we must be, and what we must become. Do not keep your eye alone on the eagle: The eagle is but the metaphor.

The Eagle: symbol of nobility and power, able to soar to altitudes inaccessible to other birds of prey, able to nest on mountain peaks, yet able to see to the valley below. The eagle: symbol of God's strength, God's power, and God's purpose.

The unfortunate reality is, however, that eagles are an endangered species. Whether in the stratosphere above or here on terra firma below, something has gone wrong. If, as I believe, the eagle is a metaphor for God, and if we are made in the image of God, and if man becomes an eagle to the extent that he mirrors in his own life who God is and thereby participates in the "eagle-ness" of God, and if we are the products of God's reproductive process, and if the species has become so scarce and so endangered that, indeed, it appears that there are no eagles—either something has disturbed the genetic process, the deoxyribonucleic acid, the DNA of the Eternal, or God Himself has become impotent and unable to reproduce those who are formed and shaped in His own likeness. If this is not so, however, tell me:

Where are the eagles—strong black men
        with vision to see beyond the moment
        and therefore are able to set the example
        as well as the agenda for our children?
Where are the eagles—virile black men who,
        in their healthy self-assurance and strength
        of character, will provide the seed and the
        security for generations yet unborn?
Where are the eagles—the strong black men who
        will marry our daughters,

and protect our women,
and guide our children?
Where are the eagles—the strong black men who
will articulate the history of our ancestors
and the hope of our progeny as much by
the pride that is in their eyes and the dignity
that is in their walk as by the words
they speak with their mouths?

There is a conduct becoming to those who are, like eagles, born and bred in the image of God.

Real Eagles are those who have learned to escape what Oliver Wendell Holmes calls "our low vaulted past."

Authentic Eagles are never content with life as it is, but are always in pursuit of life as it was meant to be.

Genuine Eagles who are always seeking, always searching, always ascending to that summit, as Gardner Calvin Taylor suggests, in the realm of the "beyondness of God."

These are eagles who understand life as a bold excursion into the unexplored, always moving toward the future, always reaching for an elusive but ineluctable eternity, always engaged in audacious flight with no assurance of safe landing.

God give us eagles who are willing, at a moment's notice, to abandon the security of familiar surroundings, who are not afraid to flirt with the foolishness of faith and who are willing to risk the phenomenon of flight with no landing pad but the platform of His promises.

Authentic eagles are an endangered species!

When Moses speaks, then, of "an eagle [who] stirreth up her nest," there is more than a suggestion here that there comes a time when the nest not only must be stirred, but must be destroyed. America takes as the symbol of her republic the American bald eagle. Yet, a close look at America today will reveal that there is something radically wrong with the nest. Whenever those who are born in the nest can no longer be fed in the nest, who must sleep in alien environments because they can find no rest in the nest, who have no political power to redevelop the nest and no economic power to co-opt the nest and no liquid assets to purchase the nest or arrange for a leveraged buyout to gain stock control of the nest—

when the nest becomes the source of one's death rather than the nurturing place for one's life, something must be done with the nest.

We thought as a result of the struggles of my generation, as a result of the protests of the sixties, that we had destroyed the nest of racism, the nest of bigotry, the nest of academic rejection and political oppression. Yet, I fear that in America a *new nest* has been constructed....

It's your turn now. The sixties have come and gone. Malcolm X is dead. Medgar Evers is dead. Martin Luther King is dead. It's your turn now to stir up America's new nests until all people live in the equality that God alone has guaranteed. It's time for the eagle to stir her nest. And not only "her" nest, but *our* nest also.

When Moses wrote his song of the eagle stirring the nest, it had to do with that event that is necessary for the maturation process of the young. It was the way by which the old eagle could say to young eagles, "It's moving time!" You see, it is possible for those who think they've "got it made" to become comfortable in the nest. A nest provides a secure environment. A nest provides the illusion that the luxuries of life are a continuing and universal phenomenon. No doubt these young but growing eagles arranged and decorated their condominium nests with the latest designer furniture. I have no question in my mind that these upwardly mobile, intellectually agile, highly motivated and college-educated young eagles hung up their degrees on the walls of the nest. They believed that because the nest was there when they got there, and because the nest had been provided free of charge—room and board, all tuition and fees, with eagle student loans taken out and paid by someone else (even with books they did not buy and did not read)—they believed that the world *owed* them a nest.

There does come a time when the eagle must stir the nest. Time for the eagle to come in with a new agenda called *personal responsibility* and *personal accountability*. Time for the eagle to come in to remind you, in the words of Frederick Douglass, "You may not get everything you work for, but you must certainly work for everything you get." You cannot stay in this nest. It is time for the eagle to come in and remind you once again of your biological and ethnic identity. The nest must be stirred.

As long as you're in the nest, you're a receiver and not a giver.

As long as you're in the nest, you're a consumer and not a producer.

As long as you're in the nest, you will absorb but you will not share.

As long as you're in the nest, you believe that the end of life is eating rather than flying.

As long as you're in the nest, you'll always eat but you'll never understand your responsibility to feed somebody else.

Perhaps more to the point, as long as you are in the nest you will have the comfort of the nest—but you will never *fly!*

What I am suggesting is that we must be the solution to our own problems. We cannot wait for the Congress or the White House or the Supreme Court to get our nest in order. We must be responsible for ourselves. We must stir up our own nest. Much as we hate to admit it, many of the problems we face in the black community have not come as the result of racism. There is something fundamentally and intellectually dishonest about those who, when caught in the vise of their own undoing, want to claim that we're in the mess we're in because we're black.

I stand on soil today made sacred by Mordecai Johnson and Benjamin Mays and Hugh Glouster and Samuel Nabrit and Louis Sullivan and Howard Thurman and T. M. Alexander and Maynard Jackson and Thomas Kilgore and Martin Luther King, and I boldly declare that your blackness is a source of your heritage and your pride and not a crutch to lean on when you can't have your way.

The nest must be stirred.

There is a great and high commission that comes with our birthright and is written in indelible ink on the diploma of this institution:

The nest must be stirred.

You cannot demand leadership of our people by special privilege, but you can earn that leadership if you walk with dignity, labor with integrity, prepare with dedication, produce with intensity, serve with selflessness, and pray with persistence and power.

You need not fear the stirring of the nest as long as you are willing to fight without fear, suffer without surrender, struggle without despair and, if need be, die without distress. It is time to stir up your nest!

There is, to be sure, implicit in the eagle metaphor of Moses a question regarding survival apart from the nest. For us, as well as for the eagle, the prospect of flight is a frightening phenomenon. For us, as well as for the eagle, the prospect of unprotected, uncharted, and unnavigated flight is to meet life head-on at some risk. Let me not disturb your exuberant joy today, students, but whatever you have studied here is not enough. No matter what your transcript says, life has some turbulent winds that your transcript cannot handle. No matter how many fellowships you have for postgraduate study, they will not shield you or save you from the wind shear of a godless and chaotic culture.

Eagles, by design of the divine and natural order, are created for flight. I realize that you have come to this high moment in your lives prepared, as it were, to fly—but do not depend overmuch on this thing called "education." Allan Bloom, in his work *The Closing of the American Mind,* has suggested that "higher education has failed democracy and failed today's students."[3] . . .

How shall you fly?

There is but one answer to my question. The answer is found with the eagle. For if the truth be known, the young had to learn to rely on the knowledge, wisdom, and power of the older eagle. That's the answer. *You will learn to fly to the extent that you learn to rely on God to teach you what the textbooks left out.* . . .

There are some things that the world of academia cannot teach you—but God can!

There are some things that sociology can never correct, and anthropology can never explain, and medicine can never cure—but God can!

There are some things that scientists will never know and that scientific method will never reveal—but God can! I still believe that God can teach some lessons that the textbooks left out.

It's not enough to know geology . . . you need to know the Rock of Ages.

It's not enough to know botany . . . you need to know the Lily of the Valley and the Rose of Sharon.

It's not enough to know zoology . . . you need to know the Lamb of God "that taketh away the sins of the world" and the One whose eye is always on the sparrow.

It's not enough to know biology ... you need to know Him who is "my life, my joy, my all."

It's not enough to know astronomy ... you need to know the one who created the sun, the moon, and the stars with His fingers, and whose heavens declare the glory of God and whose firmament shows His handiwork.

It's not enough to know gerontology ... you need to know the Ancient of Days, the First and the Last, the Alpha and the Omega, the Beginning and the End.

It's not enough to know medicine and psychology ... you need to know the heart fixer and the mind regulator.

It's not enough to know business and technology ... you need to know the Wheel in the middle of the Wheel.

The God I serve is that Eagle who stirs up the nest. You can trust Him to teach you. You can trust the Eternal. The gospel of John says, "He will guide you into all truth" (John 16:13).

You can trust Him to teach you. Solomon said, "Trust in the LORD with all thine heart; and lean not unto thine own understanding. In all thy ways acknowledge him, and he shall direct thy paths" (Prov. 3:5–6).

If you trust Him to teach you, you will fly alone and yet not alone. You see, eagles do not fly in flocks. They fly alone. They are strong and fiercely independent. They are able to make their way in pathless air. There will be those times when you, like an eagle, must travel alone.

You will not travel the common path. You will fly alone.

You will not go the way of the madding crowd. You will fly alone.

You will not follow the path of the pedestrian, or walk in the ruts of the routine. You will fly alone.

Yet you will *not* fly alone.

When the Eagle stirred up Israel's nest, Moses said, "The LORD alone did lead him, and there was no strange god with him." There are no solo flights for the child of God.

You will not travel alone.

I've seen the lightning flashing;
And heard thunder roll;

I've felt sin's breakers dashing,
Which tried to conquer my soul.
I've heard the voice of my Savior,
He bid me still fight on—
He promised never to leave me,
Never to leave me alone!

ALFRED B. SMITH

You will not fly alone. I asked Isaiah about it, and Isaiah said,

They that wait upon the LORD
shall renew their strength;
they shall mount up with wings as eagles;
they shall run, and not be weary;
and they shall walk, and not faint.

ISAIAH 40:31

You will not fly alone. I asked the hymn writer about it, and he said:

Sweet hour of prayer, sweet hour of prayer,
May I thy consolation share,
Till, from Mount Pisgah's lofty height,
I view my home, and take my flight:
This robe of flesh I'll drop, and rise
To seize the everlasting prize;
And shout, while passing thro' the air,
Farewell, farewell, sweet hour of prayer!

WILLIAM W. WALFORD

You will not fly alone. Just let that eagle stir her nest.

If the nest falls from around you and it looks as if your security structures are gone, it will be all right. It's just the eagle stirring her nest.

If the nest falls from under you and it looks as if your support system has failed, it will be all right. It's just the eagle stirring her nest.

If you don't understand what is happening, as long as you know who's making it happen, it will be all right. It's just the eagle stirring her nest. Perhaps you will understand David's prayer: "Oh that I had wings like a dove! for then would I fly away, and be at rest" (Psalm 55:6).

If you are not sure what tomorrow holds, as long as you know who holds tomorrow, it will be all right. You will not fly alone.

My language may be archaic, for we are no longer awed by the flight of birds and eagles. Ours is an age that has moved even beyond the supersonic to rockets that orbit the earth, astronauts that walk in space, satellites that transmit signals amid the shooting stars of the night. Were my language more appropriate to these times, I should say that I'm on my way to my "launching pad" and there the "Mission Control" of Eternity will be in charge of my "countdown." There, in a moment when my "window of opportunity" shall appear, in a millisecond of time, the "jet boosters" of belief will ignite and I will lift off from earth to a computer-adjusted, predetermined orbital flight path in the outer atmosphere.

But since I am just a preacher from a little country school in the backwoods of Arkansas, let me tell you how it's really going to happen:

Some glad morning when this life is o'er
I'll fly away;
To a home on God's celestial shore,
I'll fly away.

Just a few more weary days and then,
I'll fly away;
To a land where joys shall never end,
I'll fly away.

I'll fly away, O glory!
I'll fly away;
When I die, Hallelujah! By and by,
I'll fly away!

ALBERT E. BRUMLEY

For the Lord himself shall descend from heaven with a shout, with the voice of the archangel, and with the trump of God: and the dead in Christ shall rise first: Then we which are alive and remain shall be caught up together with them in the clouds, to meet the Lord in the air: and so shall we ever be with the Lord. Wherefore comfort one another with these words.

1 THESSALONIANS 4:16–18

D'RECKLY

Within the span of one's life there are so many characters, so many personalities that shape and mold one. Maybe there'll be another day when I can introduce you to Mother Staunton, who always told me, "Reverend, I'm keeping you on the altar." You need to know old Henry Taliaferro, Chairman of the Board of Trustees at Mount Ararat, who thought it his appointed duty to keep 15-watt bulbs in all the lights in the parsonage. Don't forget Betty Robinson, who rolled her eyes every Sunday to keep me in line. And one day I'll have to tell you about Mother Hardin at Mount Olivet, who, in her latter years, never quite had control of her bladder when she came to church and nearly turned every pew in Mount Olivet green before she died. But I loved Mother Hardin; she gave me my first Bible after I was ordained to preach.

I wish I had time to tell you about Deacon A. L. Lindsay who made me sit in the corner on the Sunday I came to candidate at the Metropolitan Church in Washington. You really need to know about Alice Chavies who lustily added the punctuation to every sermon with a loud, misplaced "Lord, help!" Then there was "Shoutin' Jones," who came to church every Sunday with the purposed intention of shouting no matter what did or did not happen. You should have been there the Sunday that the service was particularly dry; and when the service came to its end, exasperated, Shoutin' Jones shouted out the Spirit-filled strains of "Blessed Be the Tie That Binds."

Whenever I think of all these folks, I stand in awe of the imagination of God.

Still, you must know Aunt Sally. Her real name was Sally Matthews but we all just called her Aunt Sally. Aunt Sally lived in a little wood-frame house behind the Mount Olivet Church on Cherry Street. It was, as I recall, little more than a "shotgun" house—one of those houses that, when you opened the front door, you could see clear through to the back door.

I don't remember much about Aunt Sally's house except that she had a little pot-bellied wood-burning stove in the living room and an ice box, not a refrigerator, in her little kitchen. When Sandra and I were small, quite often we were left with Aunt Sally. At Aunt Sally's age she could only watch us, and we were really too small to get into any real trouble.

I do remember, however, that we sometimes gave Aunt Sally a "fit." Daddy was always late coming to get us, and over and over I would ask, "Aunt Sally, when is my daddy coming to get us?" Aunt Sally, for all the years I knew her, never changed her answer. Aunt Sally would always answer the question: "D'reckly! He'll be here d'reckly!"

My problem was that I didn't know what she was saying. In that day, a child did not speak back to adults. Children were, after all, to be seen and not heard. If Aunt Sally said "d'reckly," then "d'reckly" it would be. It was years later that I learned that Aunt Sally's "d'reckly" was her way of saying "directly."

All of us live in a lonely place, very often a place of our choosing. We can no more forget the place of our beginning than we could ever forget graham crackers, Ovaltine, or Absorbine Jr. Our faith has been filtered through the experience of those people who, in spite of their limitations, have nurtured us and made us available for the purifying work of the imagination of God.

The road of our life is not easy; it was not intended to be. Nevertheless, God places along the road persons who create in our minds sweet and precious memories and who open up our own imagination to wonderful worlds yet to come.

The anchored soul that will permit the death of failure will have no reason to fear. The anchored soul that is open to the possibilities of the God presence in its life will shout with the abandon of Wilson McCray and leave the shoes of hurt and pain somewhere along the roadside of life.

> *The soul that on Jesus hath leaned for repose,*
> *I will not, I will not desert to his foes.*
> *That soul though all hell should endeavor to shake,*
> *I'll never, no never, no never forsake.*

Each of us has been left in the care of an Uncle Mugga, or an Aunt Sally, or a Papa with a quarter in his hand. These are the angels God arranged for us before we were us. We have been left with an assignment to do our work, to struggle against the odds, to engage the enemy, to pursue the victory, to succeed in spite of the letters of rejection and disappointment, to remain true to the person we truly are, to remain open to the limitless possibilities of what God has imagined us to be, and to be faithful to the One in whose hand we were formed, in whose image we were made, and in whose care we yet remain. We must never forget that what we are and what we are to become remains still in God's imagination and in our own.

I have a heavenly Father who left me here with work to do. Angels are watching over me, I know. And my Savior will return to take me home to be with him. I do not know just when my Lord will come to get me, but I know that he will. Never fear, do not doubt, do not fret. All the saints of God who have gone on before—those who have loved me and taught me tenderness, those who have hated me and taught me caution, those who have been indifferent to me and taught me self-reliance—we shall all be together soon, and very soon. And, in case you wondered, my Savior will be here

D'reckly.

NOTES

INTRODUCTION

1. Howard Thurman, *Meditations of the Heart* (Richmond, IN: Harper & Row, 1976), 163.

PART ONE: IMAGINE BEGINNINGS

1. This John Updike is to be distinguished from the author of *Rabbit Run* and other books. The person I refer to was an African-American who lived in Columbus, Ohio, during the early 1950s.

2. This common-meter hymn appears as hymn no. 304 in the *National Baptist Hymn Book* (Worded Edition), published by the National Baptist Publishing Board, Nashville, Tennessee, 1906.

3. Clifton L. Taulbert, *Once Upon a Time When We Were Colored* (Tulsa, OK: Council Oak Books, 1989).

PART TWO: IMAGINE THE FAITH

1. Isaac Watts, common meter hymn. *National Baptist Hymn Book* (Nashville, TN: National Baptist Publishing Board, 1906).

2. Psalm 51:3.

3. Isaiah 1:18.

4. Psalm 51:5.

5. This is essentially a child's game, each strophe being repeated at least three times. *Mai Oui*, a French Creole phrase, is pronounced *ma-WE*.

6. James Nix, *Hold Back the Night*.

7. With the discovery of the Dead Sea Scrolls, additional writings were discovered, including the "151st Psalm," which is not included in the canon of Scripture but has been translated by Dr. Sanders.

PART THREE: IMAGINE THE CHURCH

1. Harold S. Kushner, *How Good Do We Have to Be?* (Toronto: Little, Brown, 1996), 119ff.

2. Ibid., 134–35.

3. Kushner, *How Good Do We Have to Be?*, 54.

4. Henry Nouwen, *The Wounded Healer* (Garden City, NY: Double-day, 1979).

5. Douglas Miller.

PART FOUR: IMAGINE LIFE, IMAGINE DEATH

1. Richard Bach, *Jonathan Livingston Seagull* (New York: Macmillan, 1970).

2. Adapted from a sermon preached at the baccalaureate service in the Martin Luther King Memorial Chapel, Morehouse College, Atlanta, on May 18, 1991.

3. Allan Bloom, *The Closing of the American Mind* (New York: Simon & Schuster, 1988).